Modern Techniques in a Seventeenth-Century Writer

Contemporary Critical Concepts and Pre-Enlightenment Literature

Larry Riggs
General Editor

Vol. 1

PETER LANG
New York • Washington, D.C./Baltimore
Bern • Frankfurt am Main • Berlin • Vienna • Paris

Moses Hardin

Modern Techniques in a Seventeenth-Century Writer

Anne de la Roche-Guilhen

PETER LANG
New York • Washington, D.C./Baltimore
Bern • Frankfurt am Main • Berlin • Vienna • Paris

Library of Congress Cataloging-in-Publication Data

Hardin, Moses.
Modern techniques in a seventeenth-century writer:
Anne de la Roche-Guilhen / Moses Hardin.
p. cm. — (Contemporary critical concepts and pre-Enlightenment
literature; vol. 1)
Includes bibliographical references (p.   ).
1. La Roche-Guilhen, Mlle de (Anne), 1644–1707—Technique. 2. French
fiction—17th century—History and criticism—Theory, etc. 3. Women and
literature—France—History—17th century. 4. Rhetoric—1500–1800.
5. Fiction—Technique. I. Title. II. Series.
PQ1814.L7Z73   843'.4—dc20   93-21152
ISBN 0-8204-2295-9
ISSN 1074-6781

Die Deutsche Bibliothek-CIP-Einheitsaufnahme

Hardin, Moses:
Modern techniques in a seventeenth-century writer: Anne de La Roche-
Guilhen / Moses Hardin. –New York; Washington, D.C./Baltimore; Bern;
Frankfurt am Main; Berlin; Vienna; Paris: Lang.
(Contemporary critical concepts and pre-enlightenment literature; Vol. 1)
ISBN 0-8204-2295-9
NE: GT

Cover design by James F. Brisson.

The paper in this book meets the guidelines for permanence and durability
of the Committee on Production Guidelines for Book Longevity
of the Council of Library Resources.

Printed in the United States of America.

For My Loving Wife,
Shirley Hodge Hardin

Acknowledgements

I wish to express my gratitude to everyone who helped in preparing this manuscript for publication. A special thank you to Larry Riggs (Butler University), Azzura B. Givens, Victor Carrabino, Joseph Allaire, and George Yost (Florida State University). I must also thank my wife (Shirley), and my three children (Keltrice, Eric and Jeremy) who so graciously went many hours, sometimes days, without husband or father.

Contents

Peut-être aurait-on de la peine à trouver un seul homme raisonnable qui n'ait point aimé

Anne de la Roche-Guilhen

Introduction

Anne de la Roche-Guilhen,[1] a remarkable and intriguing seventeenth-century novelist, like so many of her contemporaries, was a pioneer of the French novel. She made a substantial contribution to the development of fictional prose. Having published over twenty-five works, nearly all of which appeared in several editions, she acquired a notable following of readers during her lifetime. Many of her works were translated into English, and these translations were quite often republished. Thus, la Roche-Guilhen succeeded in capturing not only the attention of novel enthusiasts of seventeenth-century France, but an international audience as well.

Anne de la Roche-Guilhen was born around 1644 in or near Rouen and died in England, a Huguenot refugee, in 1707. She probably remained in France until around 1685, the year of the infamous revocation of the *Edit de Nantes*, for there is considerable evidence that she was in London in 1687; apparently, she remained there with two of her sisters from that year until her death. La Roche-Guilhen was born into a rather affluent family of Protestant nobility, but after her father's death in 1682 it appears that the family fortune had been depleted. This dramatic change in her financial status is evidenced by the fact that while in

England, she and her sisters, Marie and Madeleine, received benefits from the Royal Bounty, a financial aid program for the Huguenot refugees. Undoubtedly, Anne de la Roche-Guilhen was forced to write in order to support her family.

When compared to other seventeenth-century novelists, la Roche-Guilhen is rather unique. Most of her works were written while she was in exile, and it seems that she never had the honor of mingling with those who frequented the famous *salons* of seventeenth-century France. Unlike many of her contemporaries, la Roche-Guilhen did not have close ties with any of the great writers of her day. Consequently, the success of her novels depended solely upon their personal merit. Nevertheless, la Roche-Guilhen was indeed a gifted writer for, based upon the number of editions of her publications, her works never lacked an audience.

On the contrary, other seventeenth-century novelists, although they too had their problems, did not suffer the degradation of being outcasts as did la Roche-Guilhen; they were not only able to live rather peacefully in their native country, but also many of them gained acceptance into the elite literary and social circles. Mlle de Scudéry, for example, was surrounded by friends such as Madame de Sévigné, Madame de Rambouillet and Conrart and became so popular that eventually she opened her own *salon*.

Madame de Villedieu also had rather easy access into the literary world. The Duchesse de Montbazon was the *protectrice* of Madame de Villedieu's family, the Desjardins. Thus, through her connection with the Montbazon family, Madame de Villedieu, at the age of fifteen, was reading her poetry in the *salon* of her protectress.

Madame de La Fayette shared many of the acquaintances of Mlle de Scudéry and Mme de Villedieu, but more importantly, she had ties with Henriette d'Angleterre. It was due to this friendship that Madame de La Fayette had free access to the royal court. She frequented the salon of Mlle de Scudéry and the "Hôtel de Rambouillet." Moreover,

Le public du XVIIe siècle et les historiens se sont accordés à considérer que les romans de Mme de La Fayette étaient en fait une oeuvre collective. Il est certain que Gilles Ménage, Segrais, Huet et La Rochefoucauld y eurent quelque part. (Niderst 35)

Conquering adverse conditions and leaving her homeland in search of religious freedom, la Roche-Guilhen did not forget her French readers, nor did she ignore the fact that love played an important role in the discussions in the famous *salons* in France, and that it was often the subject matter of novels of her day. Consequently, she wrote only about the love affairs of princes and princesses. In her novels la Roche-Guilhen portrays love as an extremely powerful force that captures its victims, causing them to act irrationally, and inevitably gives rise to wars and murders. Once love-stricken, the hero is eternally held prisoner by his captor.

The helpless state of la Roche-Guilhen's characters prefigures the ideology of twentieth-century existentialism—God is dead; existence is confrontation with others; existence is tragic. The existence of la Roche-Guilhen's personages is indeed tragic. Once they have been struck by Cupid's arrow, they almost immediately fall into a deep melancholic state, and being in each other's presence only increases their sorrow. The hero and heroine are in love, but they are unable to find happiness together without experiencing a sort of Pascalian anguish. Based upon their inability to find happiness, it seems that God has denied them his grace.

Anne de la Roche-Guilhen explains in the preface to *Le Grand Scanderberg* that the mystical powers of love are unavoidable. She also reminds us that it was love that overwhelmed great conquerors and heroes like Alexander, Caesar and Hercules. She adds that "Mars même, le Dieu de Guerre, ne put résister aux attraits de la Déesse des Graces & des Amours; & il se croyait trop heureux de partager avec Vulcain les faveurs de Venus" (la Roche-Guilhen 3-4). Though it also played an important role in the works of other seventeenth-century novelists, la Roche-Guilhen's treatment of love is extraordinary. In the works of writers like La Calprenède and Madame de Villedieu, love is portrayed in a rather abstract manner. These two authors were preoccupied with conventions such as military battles, shipwrecks, recognitions and trips to foreign lands; consequently, love was forced to play a secondary role.

With Mlle de Scudéry and Madame de La Fayette, love made strides toward the forefront. Mlle de Scudéry treats love from an analytical perspective, for it becomes the topic of her numerous interminable discussions. In fact, ". . . Mlle de Scudéry est en avance d'un siècle par la matière dont elle analyse les rêveries douces et mélancoliques auxquelles s'abandonnent les âmes sensibles" (Lever 132). Likewise, Mme de La Fayette's treatment of love is analytical, but she goes a step further, examining the psychological development of her heroine, Madame de Clèves.

Anne de la Roche-Guilhen, who neither analyzes love in long discussions nor delves into the psychological state of its victims, depicts love as a mighty demigod who swoops down to attack his prey without warning. Thus, her heroes often fall in love at first sight of a beautiful princess; sometimes they are stricken by love as soon as the heroine's voice is heard. It is remarkable that la Roche-Guilhen, who apparently was not afforded many of life's pleasures, was able to paint such a passionate picture of love.

Mademoiselle de la Roche-Guilhen did not write the ten-volume novel that was so popular during the first half of the seventeenth century. Her individual works usually contain less than two hundred pages and were always published in their entirety. Characteristically, the action involves a hero (usually a prince) who falls in love with the most beautiful princess in the land—she is sometimes a captive or slave; he must, however, overcome many obstacles before obtaining the freedom to marry his beloved. In short, her prose fiction may be classified as historical, heroic, gallant or tragic, for frequently one finds a mixture of historic facts, heroic or gallant deeds and death. Although Anne de la Roche-Guilhen undeniably succeeded with the novelistic form, she also courageously explored another literary genre resulting in the publication of a musical verse play.

Seemingly, la Roche-Guilhen decided to wait until the last years of her life before lashing out at the Catholics who, with the revocation of the Edict of Nantes, had brutally and abruptly robbed her of the right to worship God freely. She did not aim her fiery darts at the laymen, but at those of the highest rank in the church hierarchy. These vindictive attacks were made in her *Histoires des favorites* (1697). In the story entitled *Histoire de Marozie*, la Roche-Guilhen replaces the Pope's chastity with an insatiable lust for women. Inevitably, the Pope gets married. In the *Histoire de Julie de Farnèse*, the author is so malicious in her assault against Popes that the abbé de La Porte declares:

> Je ne vous déguiserait point, Madame, que cette Histoire est un tissu d'invectives contres les Papes, & contres les gens d'Eglise. Mademoiselle de la Rocheguilhem, qui sans doute étoit Protestante, donne une carrière à son esprit satyrique & railleur; mais elle est quelquefois insipide à force de vouloir être plaisante. (La Porte 3:80)

Anne de la Roche-Guilhen's life is a mysterious labyrinth, for little has been published about her during the period from shortly after her birth (1644) until exactly thirty years later (1674) when her first literary work appeared. Historians have produced nothing about her youth and very little about her life in general. However, considering what is known about her today, it appears that she led a very difficult life.

The seventeenth century has engendered many rather recent studies of the novel of the time.[2] Nevertheless, only a few of them mention la Roche-Guilhen. René Godenne's *Histoire de la nouvelle française aux XVIIe et XVIIIe siècles* (1970) refers to the author and her novels quite frequently. La Roche-Guilhen's literary compositions are most often cited as examples of the various types of novels, the *nouvelle historique* or *nouvelle galante* for example. Godenne usually alludes to la Roche-Guilhen as she relates to other seventeenth-century novelists, but he does not examine her originality, nor does he attempt to explain the role she played in the development of the French novel. In Godenne's *Histoire de la nouvelle française . . .*, one finds statements such as "les romanciers, les nouvellistes manifestent un goût très vif de commencer leur intrigue *in medias res*. Par example, les premières pages du *Grand Scanderberg* (1688) de Mlle de la Roche-Guilhem [sic]" (108).

Anne de la Roche-Guilhen is also mentioned, though not as often as in Godenne, in English Showalter, Junior's *The Evolution of the French Novel 1641-1782* (1972). Like Godenne, Showalter makes no effort to analyze la Roche-Guilhen's novels. He simply indicates that Mademoiselle de la Roche-Guilhen, along with other seventeenth-century writers, realized that the popularity of the "roman" was on the decline (13-14, 17), that she, in the prefaces to some of her works, declared that her novels were not fiction (17-18), and that she used the names of foreign countries in her literary compositions without the slightest description of the scenery (145-146).

Alexandre Calame's *Anne de la Roche-Guilhen, romancière huguenote 1644-1707* (1972), however, is perhaps the most complete study of Anne de la Roche-Guilhen's life and works. He uncovered documents, including her baptismal records, that prove she spent time in London. The results of his research clarify many of the mysteries about la Roche-Guilhen's life, but there are still unanswered questions. Calame's treatment of Mademoiselle de la Roche-Guilhen is limited to her various publications, the authenticity of their authorship and certain aspects of her life. He not only lists the different editions, but he also explains the changes that were made in each. Basically, he gives a short synopsis of each work; but, more importantly, he compiles a complete and reliable list of Anne de la Roche-Guilhen's works.

More recently, Anne de la Roche-Guilhen is mentioned in Joan DeJean's *Tender Geographies: Women and the Origins of the Novel in France*, but only as one of the "novelists less known today but very prolific and celebrated in their time" (128). La

Roche-Guilhen's name also appears in two footnotes. The first note is a reference to "the intellectuals who . . . blended into the Protestant diaspora . . . denouncing the French system" (129); it cites her "staunch" Protestant background and the addition of "La Roche" to the family name. The second note refers to the new connotation (sexual liaisons) of the word *galant* in the seventeenth-century novel. After a long explanation of Scudery's use of the term, it reveals that " . . . in her *Sapho, ou l'heureuse inconstance* (1695), La Roche-Guilhem notes that the women of Lesbos 'appeared *galantes* without endangering their virtue' (6)."

Since the main purpose of this study is to analyze the novelistic techniques (plot, characterization and narration) in the works of la Roche-Guilhen, no effort has been made to add to what Calame and other scholars have published concerning her life and publications. Therefore, to a great extent, the author relies on Calame's scholarly publication for information on la Roche-Guilhen's life.

Thus far, American critics of seventeenth-century French literature have failed to search for any particular form of originality in Anne de la Roche-Guilhen and have considered her only as an imitator of Madeleine de Scudéry. In one of his letters, abbé de La Porte goes so far as to say that one of the author's works, *L'Histoire de Roxelène*, ". . . n'est qu'une répétition de ce que Mademoiselle de Scudéri [sic] nous apprend de cette Princesse fameuse dans son *Illustre Bassa*" (81). Hence, in this study, particular emphasis will be placed on the differences and similarities in the works of these two authors, Madeleine de Scudéry and Anne de la Roche-Guilhen, in order to prove that there is indeed originality in la Roche-Guilhen.

La Roche-Guilhen's uniqueness is revealed in the special manner in which she treats love, plot, characterization and narration. Anne de la Roche-Guilhen's characters are portrayed as beings predestined to live tragic lives—a Jansenist belief. In the end, however, these seemingly condemned personages are set free (either by the mysterious *deus ex machina* or by the sword).

La Roche-Guilhen's narrative style is original in that she affords her characters the opportunity to tell and listen to stories.

Seemingly, there is a mania for stories. Granted that other novelists used many of the same devices as la Roche-Guilhen, there is a marked difference in how these techniques are applied. This examination of plot, characterization and narration is in essence an effort to analyze la Roche-Guilhen's novelistic techniques in order to uncover her originality. In an effort to establish the role Anne de la Roche-Guilhen played in the development of the French novel, she is compared mainly to Scudèry, but her works are also compared to those of other seventeenth-century writers.

This analysis, however, is limited to three novels: *Almanzaïde* (1674), *Le Grand Scanderberg* (1688) and *Zingis* (1711). These three works were selected mainly because they represent not only three decades during which our author published, but three phases. For example, in *Almanzaïde*, love is portrayed as a domineering force, while in *Le Grand Scanderberg*, it is honor and duty that reign supreme. In *Zingis*, emphasis is placed on the difficulty of choosing duty over love. Although there are few in *Almanzaïde*, the popular seventeenth-century conventions such as military battles and kidnappings emerge progressively in the latter two novels. *Almanzaïde* was Mademoiselle de la Roche-Guilhen's first novel to be published. *Le Grand Scanderberg* appeared fourteen years later. Although *Zingis* was first published in 1691, the 1711 edition is used for our analysis, since the various editions do not differ significantly. An analysis of these three works, *Almanzaïde*, *Le Grand Scanderberg* and *Zingis*, also discloses any important modifications in la Roche-Guilhen's style.

The aforementioned novels were also chosen because the authenticity of their authorship has never been challenged. Of the twenty-five works published by Mademoiselle de la Roche-Guilhen, the authorship of eight is still uncertain (Calame 91-94). The author, like other seventeenth-century writers, was a victim of the avaricious publishers who printed books with the name that would produce the most sales.

Surely such a prolific author as Anne de la Roche-Guilhen, one whose works were in such great demand during her lifetime, is worthy of the attention of modern seventeenth-century critics. For too long, la Roche-Guilhen's literary accomplishments have been unjustly neglected, and an in-depth analysis of her literary compositions is long overdue. This study was conceived as an effort to establish la Roche-Guilhen in her rightful place in the development of the French novel, to introduce her to those American seventeenth-century critics who have not heard of her, and to encourage critics everywhere to discover the vast unexplored territory of French literature of the seventeenth century. It is hoped that this work will inspire a joint effort among modern critics to exhume the author from dusty shelves and moth-eaten documents.[3]

Chapter One

The Life and Works of
Anne de la Roche-Guilhen

Much like that of her characters, the life of Anne de la Roche-Guilhen is shrouded in mystery. Although records of her birth and death have been found, details about her education, her familial environment, her marital status and her physical characteristics are still undetermined.

For many years, the uncertainty of la Roche-Guilhen's date of birth led to the publication of several erroneous dates. The *Nouvelle biographie générale* and Cardinal George Grente's *Dictionnaire des lettres françaises* both state that she was born in 1640. According to the *Biographie universelle*, she was born around 1653. L'Abbé de la Porte, in his *Histoire littéraire des femmes françaises*, places her birth in 1663. The *Biographie universelle, ancienne et moderne* states that one may only estimate her date of birth based on publication of her first work, which appeared in 1674. Obviously, it was presumed that Anne de la Roche-Guilhen must have been at least twenty-one years old when she wrote her first novel, for 1653 is given in the *Biographie universelle, ancienne et moderne* as the year of her birth. The above year is footnoted with

Si l'on plaçait comme l'abbé de la Porte, la naissance de

Mlle de la Roche-Guilhen à l'an 1663, il faudrait en conclure qu'elle avait l'esprit très précoce puisqu'elle aurait publié son premier ouvrage à douze ans. (316)

For many years, scholars neglected to verify the year Anne de la Roche-Guilhen was born. Those authors (Cardinal George Grentes, La Porte, etc.) who gave a certain year as her date of birth were content to publish dates derived from mere assumptions and, as a result, the public was forced to draw its own conclusions based on a list of inaccurate dates.

Finally, in his *Anne de la Roche-Guilhen, romancière huguenote 1644-1707* (1972), Alexandre Calame eliminates much of the confusion with regard to la Roche-Guilhen's date of birth. Although he does not actually state that she was born in 1644, he gives that particular year as the year of her birth in the title of his book. Evidently, Calame drew this conclusion because he had found records showing that Anne de la Roche-Guilhen was baptized on July 24, 1644 in the parish of Quevilly. This date is substantiated by Alexandre Cioranescu in his *Bibliographie de la littérature française du dix-septième siècle*. Nevertheless, it cannot be accepted as an absolute fact, for though the Huguenots of seventeenth-century France did not immediately change the Catholic practice of infant baptism, it is not certain, but only quite probable, that she was baptized the year she was born. With the discovery of la Roche-Guilhen's records of baptism, it is certain that she was born during or before the year 1644.

Familial Background

Anne de la Roche-Guilhen was the oldest of five girls. There was also a brother who was stillborn and buried on June 13, 1643. Her sisters, Marie, Esther, Elisabeth and Madeleine were baptized respectively in 1646, 1647, 1648 and 1652.

Anne and her four sisters were the daughters of Charles de Guilhen and Marie-Anne d'Azemar. The lives of Charles and Marie-Anne are as mysterious as that of their eldest daughter.

Charles de Guilhen died in 1682. At that time, the death announcement claimed that he was sixty-eight years old. If this pronouncement is true, he was born in 1614. He was recognized as a member of the Huguenot nobility. Charles's father was called the Sieur de la Roche. "La Roche est un lieu -- dit à quelque deux kilomètres au nord-est de Baix en Ardeche" (Calame 11-12). Baix, a Huguenot stronghold, was captured in 1622 by Lesdiquière, who completely destroyed its defenses; another siege took place in 1628. It was perhaps after the latter siege of Baix (1628) that Charles de Guilhen, only fourteen years old at the time, left Vivarais and went to Normandy. Nevertheless, the announcement of the engagement (November 24, 1641) and marriage (October 1, 1642) of Charles de Guilhen with Marie-Anne d'Azemar was found in the registers of the parish in Quevilly, a suburb where the Protestant church of Rouen was located (Calame 9-10).

Thus, Charles de Guilhen was quite involved in the Huguenot struggle which took place in France during the seventeenth century. Apparently, he witnessed the two attacks on Baix, and was probably given a biased explanation of what was really taking place. Undoubtedly, Charles shared his prejudicial opinions of the Catholics with his daughters.

The family of Marie-Anne d'Azemar, la Roche-Guilhen's mother, was also of the Huguenot nobility. Originally from the South, the Azemars were glassmakers. Their factory, Saint Sever, acquired in 1619, was located in Rouen; it was a very important addition to the Azemar Family. For many years, it held exclusive rights to all glassmaking in the Rouen area, a privilege that was lost while Marie-Anne's three brothers were in control of the company.

Marie-Anne d'Azemar, baptized on March 8, 1620 in the Protestant church of Rouen-Quevilly, was born into a family that had ties with well-known literary figures. Her mother's eldest brother was the famous poet Saint-Amant. One of the sisters of Marie-Anne d'Azemar married a distant relative of Tallemant des Réaux, making Saint-Amant the great-uncle of Anne de la Roche-Guilhen, and Tallemant des Réaux her relative by marriage.

Mysterious Years in London

During her youth, Anne de la Roche-Guilhen was exposed to the tumultuous plight of the Huguenots of seventeenth-century France. It appears that she, along with her family, was constantly seeking refuge. La Roche-Guilhen, as well as two of her sisters, finally found refuge in London, England, where she apparently spent the last twenty years of her life:

> A partir de 1687 et jusqu'à sa mort, survenue en 1707, nous savons de source sûre que Mademoiselle de la Roche-Guilhen habita Londres, mais la date de son départ de Rouen est moins facile à établir. Sa famille habite encore à Rouen en 1664 à la mort de sa mère mais c'est à Paris que meurt son père en 1682. En 1685 pourtant, son oncle Pierre d'Azemar est encore à la tête de la verrerie familiale de Saint-Sever. C'est d'autre part en 1682-83 que le libraire Claude Barbin publie à Paris les trois volumes de son *Histoire des guerres civiles de Grenade*. A partir de cette date toutes les oeuvres de Mademoiselle de la Roche-Guilhen furent publiées par des libraires de Hollande. On serait donc tenté de penser que c'est à la révocation de l'Edit de Nantes, en 1685, que notre romancière se refugia à Londres, en compagnie de ses deux soeurs. (Calame 29)

After 1683, all of Mademoiselle de la Roche-Guilhen's works were published exclusively in Holland. Apparently, it was this fact that led several scholars to believe that she lived in Holland for a period of time. The *Biographie générale* states that ". . . elle [Anne de la Roche-Guilhen] appartenait à une bonne famille protestante et habitait Paris à l'époque de la révocation de l'édit de Nantes; elle se refugia en Hollande, d'où, en 1697, elle passa en Angleterre" (661). According to the *Biographie générale*, Mlle de la Roche-Guilhen spent approximately twelve years in Holland, after the revocation of the *Edit de Nantes*, before going on to England. Michaud, in his *Biographie universelle*, goes so far as to suggest that once Anne de la Roche-Guilhen arrived in Holland, she remained there until her death: "Il parait que Mlle de la Roche-guilhem habita Paris jusqu'à la révocation de l'édit de Nantes, et qu'alors elle se retire en Hollande . . . " (316). In view of the fact that all of la Roche-Guilhen's works were published in Holland after 1683, it apears that she indeed lived in Holland for a while, but there is no real proof that she actually lived or died there.

The hypotheses of the *Biographie générale* and the *Biographie universelle* become questionable when one realizes that a play, a musical comedy, entitled *Rare en tout* was presented and published in London in 1677. This play contained a dedicatory epistle which was signed by la Roche-Guilhen. The mere fact that Anne de la Roche-Guilhen is the author of a play published and presented in England does not prove that she actually lived there. However, a decree given by King Charles II substantiates the presumption that she spent some time in England. In this decree, the king orders the royal musicians to rehearse the music for the "French comedy" at any time that Anne de la Roche-Guilhen and Paisible request that they do so:

> Un ordre du roi Charles II date du 5 février 1677 ordonne de préparer pour la troupe le théâtre de Whitehall et un autre ordre du 22 mai prescrit aux musiciens royaux "to practise in the theatre at Whitehall at such tymes as Madam Le Roch and Mr. Paisible [Jacques Paisible, a French musician] shall apoint for ye practiceing of such musik as is to be in ye French comedy". (Calame 30)

Provided that "Madam Le Roch" is in reality Mlle de la Roche-Guilhen, she was in England in 1677 when Charles II gave the above order.

There is other documentation which seems to prove that Anne de la Roche-Guilhen lived in England for several years—possibly from 1677 until her death (1707). La Roche-Guilhen's *Rare en tout* was dedicated to La duchesse de Grafton, who knew la Roche-

Guilhen well. As a matter of fact, Mademoiselle de la Roche-Guilhen may have been the duchess' companion or French tutor. Since two of Mlle de la Roche-Guilhen's works, *Almanzaïde* and *Astérie*, were translated into English in 1678 and 1677, respectively, (another English version in 1680), and since *Astérie* inspired Saunders, a poet of the Westminister school, to write a tragedy (based on *Astérie*), it is even more plausible that la Roche-Guilhen lived in England at that time.

Nevertheless, the hypothesis that Mlle de la Roche-Guilhen was living in England all of this time is contradicted by the fact that Anne and her two sisters received aid which was given to the victims of the revocation of the *Edit de Nantes*. Normally, a person who had already lived in England for ten years would not have been eligible to receive this aid. It is possible that Anne de la Roche-Guilhen was in fact in England after around 1677 and was joined later by her sisters, Marie and Madeleine.

One of Anne de la Roche-Guilhen's works, *Les Guerres civiles de Grenade*, was published in Paris in 1682-83. This publication further contradicts the assumption that la Roche-Guilhen lived in England from the time of her participation in the production of *Rare en tout* until her death; however, Calame perceives the publication of *Les Guerres civiles de Grenade* as further proof that his hypothesis is conclusive. He indicates that it is quite possible that the publisher, Barbin, kept the manuscript for several years before printing it:

> La publication à Paris des *Guerres civiles de Grenade* en 1682-83 ne contredit pas notre hypothèse, au contraire, si Barbin possédait le manuscrit depuis plusieurs années et le publia en l'absence de l'auteur, cela expliquerait qu'il y ait maintenu une dédicace au marquis de la Fuente, ambassadeur d'Espagne qui avait quitté Paris depuis plus de seize ans et était mort depuis dix. (Calame 32)

Obviously, Anne de la Roche-Guilhen did indeed spend the last years of her life in England. According to the records of the

"Royal Bounty" (Calame 35), financial aid was given to Anne and her sisters, Marie and Madeleine. Furthermore, these records indicate that Marie and Madeleine were sickly, that they were from Rouen and resided on Panton Street (in London), and that one of the sisters, Madeleine, died around 1700. Marie died in 1703 and Anne in 1707. Based on records of payment for funerals, the three sisters were also buried in England.

Clearly, Anne de la Roche-Guilhen's life was not peaceful. She was born into a noble Huguenot family, but because of its involvement in the religious struggles of seventeenth-century France, she was not in a position to enjoy fully her social status. Anne and her family had to relocate several times, seemingly, in a vain attempt to find refuge in France. Finally, la Roche-Guilhen sought a tranquil home in England, where, no longer financially secure, she was forced to write for monetary gain.

Presently, there is no indication that la Roche-Guilhen experienced the romatic life she always wrote about. There was no handsome prince in her life to kidnap her and take her away from her family problems, giving her happiness ever after. On the contrary, she apparently never married.

Anne de la Roche-Guilhen, it appears, experienced those pleasures vicariously through her characters. While she had to spend a lot of her time at home with her ill sisters, la Roche-Guilhen sweeps her heroes and heroines off to faraway, exotic places like Mexico, Africa and China; while she found no one with whom to share her life, her heroines always have handsome princes to rescue them from their loneliness; while la Roche-Guilhen was poor, her heroes and heroines, though they may appear to be nothing more than slaves at first, are always the sons and daughters of wealthy kings.

Authorship Questioned

During her lifetime, Anne de la Roche-Guilhen wrote and published many literary works. Twenty-five publications have been attributed to her. During the seventeenth centry, however, the literary creations of many writers were habitually included in the collections of other authors. La Roche-Guilhen was not an exception to this trend; several of her novels appeared in lists of the publications of other authors. The listed works of Madame de Villedieu contained *Astérie ou Tamerlan*, *Journal amoureux d'Espagne*, and *Histoire des guerres civiles de Grenade*. *Le Journal amoureux d'Espagne* was also attributed to Mme de La Fayette. The authorship of some of the novels that have been credited to la Roche-Guilhen is therefore still the object of research.

In 1960, Marc Chadourne published an article in which he attributes *Le Journal amoureux d'Espagne* to Madame de La Fayette. Immediately, critics responded to this presumption with attempts to prove its invalidity. Mme Aldbais and Micheline Cuénin refuted Marc Chadourne's attribution of *Le Journal amoureux d'Espagne* to Madame de La Fayette, but they did not assign it to Anne de la Roche-Guilhen. A few years after the publication of Marc Chadourne's article, Madame Aldbais published an article in which she ". . . prétendit démontrer, avec des arguments de critique interne, c'est-à-dire stylistiques, que le roman est de Mme de Villedieu" (Calame 23). In 1970, Micheline Cuénin published an article in the same literary journal. She pointed out that the grammar and vocabulary used by Madame Aldbais to support her theory that *Le Journal amoureux d'Espagne* was written by Mme de Villedieu were commonly used in all narrative prose of that epoch. The authorship of *Le Journal amoureux d'Espagne* remains uncertain.

Chronological List of Works

Because Anne de la Roche-Guilhen is unknown to many modern critics, a complete list of her works, along with a plot summary in most cases, is included in this study.

In 1674, Mlle de la Roche-Guilhen's first novel, *Almanzaïde*, was published. *Almanzaïde* gives an account of the conflict that develops between two Moroccan brothers who are in love with the same woman, Almanzaïde. One of the brothers (the one Almanzaïde prefers), learns that his rival is in fact his brother and that Almanzaïde is his sister. All is not lost, however; he soon discovers that Almanzaïde is not his sister after all; later it is discovered that she is the rightful heir to the throne of a nearby country. They get married and, when they return to her country and their new home, Almanzaïde receives the crown and places it on the head of her new husband.

Apparently, la Roche-Guilhen was writing well before 1674, for she not only published her first novel (*Almanzaïde*) in 1674 along with the first two volumes of the second, *Arioviste*, but in 1675, she published the last two volumes of her second novel as well as her third novel. *Arioviste* depicts the military conquests of Jules César, who finally defeats Arioviste, the king of the Germans. For the most part, the action centers around these kings' rivalry for the love of the beautiful Vociane. Once Agatie, the queen (wife of Arioviste), discovers that Vociane loves Arioviste, she makes plans to force Vociane to marry Divitiac, a high ranking soldier, but her plans never materialize. When Agatie realizes that her efforts are in vain, she becomes ill and dies. Shortly thereafter, Vociane is kidnapped, but Arioviste puts the culprit to flight and finally has Vociane all to himself.

The third novel, *Astérie ou Tamerlan*, was published daily over a period of months; the last pages appeared in 1675. This is the first of Mlle de la Roche-Guilhen's works to be attributed to Mme de Villedieu. It, among others, was included in the 1702 edition of *Oeuvres de Mme de Villedieu*. There is little doubt, however, that this novel was written by la Roche-Guilhen, for she signed its dedicatory epistle. Tamerlan's two sons, Thémir and Adanaxe, are in love with Astérie. Thus, Thémir and his governor, Odmar, plot against Adanaxe. Ultimately, Odmar tries to kill Adanaxe but ends up killing Thémir, and confesses that Thémir was actually his son whom he had switched with the real prince who died at birth. Hence, Adanaxe is the sole heir. He marries Astérie.

During the very same year (1675), still another novel attributed to Anne de la Roche-Guilhen was made public. This time, however, the publication takes place in Holland, whereas all of her previous works were published in France. The title of the novel is *Le Journal amoureux d'Espagne*. It tells the story of the love life of Isabelle, one of the main characters. Dom Guzman and Dom Ramir are both in love with Isabelle, but she loves Dom Alphonse. Influenced by the suggestion of a friend, Ramir reluctantly decides to kill Alphonse. While reserving a place in her heart for Alphonse, Isabelle marries Dom Ramir. However, she soon becomes remorseful and begins to hate her husband. Heeding the advice of friends, she leaves the country. Dom Ramir follows her, only to die at the hands of pirates while attempting to free her. Isabelle dies (of chagrin and sadness) soon thereafter.

In 1677, Mlle de la Roche-Guilhen's only play, *Rare en tout*, was published and performed in London. This three-act musical comedy, written in verse, is a mixture of music and ballet. It begins with a prologue, composed of 106 verses, which is about one-half the length of each of the three acts. The prologue, like much of the play, consists mainly of songs performed by a chorus, a soloist, and a trio. The first act begins with a lengthy monologue (100 lines) in which La Treille, the valet, seems to set the stage for the remainder of the play. The plot revolves around Rare en tout, a character who has left France to come to England in search of his beloved. He finds her, only to fall in love with another. He sings his way into the heart of his new-found mistress but loses her when she overhears his heartless words about love. The evolution of the plot depends largely upon the main characters' "mania for music" (Spire Pitou 358).

Le Comte d'Essex is another novel that has been attributed to la Roche-Guilhen; however, its authorship is still uncertain. This publication has been assigned to our author solely because Paul Marret, one of la Roche-Guilhen's publishers, included it in his *Catalogue des ouvrages de Mademoiselle de la Rocheguilhem*, which is found in the 1703 edition of *Histoire des favorites*. Unfortunately, my attempts to secure a copy of this novel or a summary of its plot have been unsuccessful. It is certainly a point to be pursued later.

Histoires des guerres civiles de Grenade, another novel written by Anne de la Roche-Guilhen, was first published in 1683; a second edition with the title *Aventures grenadines* appeared in 1710. The action takes place in the kingdom of Grenada where the citizens, Spanish Moors, are divided into two social classes. The development of the action depends largely upon the conflict among the citizens of Grenada. During one of the many periods of unrest, the kingdom is invaded; the king of Grenada is defeated and sent to Africa. This novel contains many duels and military games, along with extraordinary spectacles of pageantry.

In 1687, *Zamire* was published. It appeared in a second edition in 1692. This is yet another novel that has been attributed to Anne de la Roche-Guilhen without substantial proof that she actually wrote it. In the preface of the 1687 edition, the reader is told that the manuscript was given to the publisher by a stranger and that there was no reason to doubt its authorship. On the other hand, *Zamire* could have been written by François Raguenet, who is supposedly also the author of *Syroés et Mirame*. The latter novel, except for a few differences in style and the addition of another story at the end, is nothing more than a reproduction of *Zamire*. This seems to suggest that François Raguenet wrote the first edition of *Zamire*, later made some changes in it, and published it again under the title *Syroés et Mirame*. Or did he plagiarize?

In 1688, *Le Grand Scanderberg*, another novel by Anne de la Roche-Guilhen, appeared. Other editions followed in 1692 and 1711; an English translation, *The Great Scanderberg*, was published in 1690 and yet another, *Scanderberg the Great*, was issued to the public in 1721 and again in 1729. *Le Grand Scanderberg* is about the love life of an Albanian prince whose name at birth is George. However, he is surrendered, as a hostage, to the sultan who gives him the Moslem name Scander (Alexander). In addition to the name Scander, he is given the title Beg, which later becomes Berg because it is sometimes misunderstood. Scanderberg escapes in revolt against the sultan, leads the army of the Albanians (his people), reclaims his Christian faith and, before his death, leads his army to many victories over the

Turkish people. Though military battles are prevalent, love plays an important role in the development of the action in this novel. In the preface, the reader is told that the gallant Scanderberg, though he was in love, never allowed love to make him do or say anything that is not worthy of a man of his stature.

Intrigues amoureuses de quelques anciens grecs was published in 1690. Its attribution to la Roche-Guilhen is based solely on its appearance on the list published by Paul Marret in 1703. Thus, it is not certain that she is in fact its author, for Marret's catalogue is not completely reliable. In the *Intriques amoureuses de quelques anciens grecs*, "il s'agit du mariage de Socrate et de Xantipe et de la rivaltié d'Alcibiade et de Philoclès pour l'amour de la belle Hyparette" (Calame 45).

In 1691, Anne de la Roche-Guilhen published *Zingis*, a novel that was especially popular during the years immediately following. The very next year (1692) both a French version and an English translation entitled *Taxila* appeared. *Zingis* was also included in the *Nouvelles historiques* (1692 edition), re-edited in 1711 and included in the third volume of the *Histoires tragiques et galantes* (1723). In the 1711 edition, Anne de la Roche-Guilhen is indicated as the author. Therefore, there is no valid reason to question the authorship of *Zingis*.

Zingis is a love story filled with many of the elements often found in the novels of the seventeenth century: kidnappings, duels, disguises, recognitions, and other dramatic devices. The action takes place in the exotic Cambalu, which is the name given to Pekin. The action revolves around the two main characters: Zingis, the son of the *Mongules*, and Taxila, the daughter of the khan of Tartary. After overcoming many obastacles, Zingis and Taxila, along with two other couples, get married.

In 1691, the same year *Zingis* was published, another work by Anne de la Roche-Guilhen, *Nouvelles historiques*, appeared. There are three novels (really novelettes) in this particular edition: *Gaston Phébus, Comte de Foix, la Prédiction accomplie* and *Les Deux Fortunes imprévues*. *Gaston Phébus* is about the rivalry between a father, the *comte de Foix*, and his two sons, Bernard and Gaston, for the young princess Isabelle. The father has the younger son, Gaston, killed. Nevertheless, just when he thinks he will be able to lead a happy, trouble-free life, Bernard, his older son, takes Isabelle to Castile, where he marries her.

La Prédiction accomplie is, as the title suggests, about a prediction that comes true. A father, Fabrice, learns from an astrologer that his son, Silvio, is destined to obtain a high position. Fearing that Silvio will replace him as king, Fabrice has his son thrown into the sea; however, the young man is rescued by Sicilians. He then serves in the court of Sicily and marries Diane, the heiress of the Sicilian throne. Fabrice learns that Silvio is alive and tells Silvio that he is not his son after all. Another edition of *La Prédiction accomplie* was published in 1732. This edition, however, was entitled *l'Horoscope accompli, nouvelle sicilienne*. The name of the hero was changed from Silvio to Frédéric. Otherwise, there were few modifications in the text of the 1732 edition.

The action of the third novel, *Les Deux Fortunes imprévues*, takes place in the mountains of *Jaca*. It is about two women and the difficulties they encouter while trying to find their respective lovers. They are finally reunited.

Le Duc de Guise, Another novel attributed to the pen of Anne de la Roche-Guilhen, was made public for the first time in 1693. It depicts the love affair between the duc de Guise and Madame de Villequier. The latter is finally stabbed by her jealous husband. *Le Duc de Guise* was also included in the third volume of the *Histoires tragiques et galantes*, published in 1723.

Histoire chronologique d'Espagne appeared for the first time in 1694 with the title *Histoire chronologique d'Espagne, commençant à l'origine des premiers habitants du pays; tirée de Mariana et des plus célèbres auteurs espagnols. Par Mademoiselle****. The title suggests that this historical work is based on the works of Spanish authors. Evidently, Anne de la Roche-Guilhen based this work on the *Inventaire général de l'histoire d'Espagne*, which is an extract from Mariana, Turquet and others. This work was published in several other editions, and an English translation was included in

1724.   The English title, like the French title, gives a good indication of its contents: *The History of the royal genealogy of Spain.*

Histoire des amours du duc d'Arione was published in 1694. It has a Spanish setting with the action taking place in the fifteenth century.   It has been accredited to Mlle de la Roche-Guilhen because of its inclusion on Marret's list (works of Anne de la Roche-Guilhen).

In 1694, la Roche-Guilhen's *L'Innocente justifiée* was published.   A second edition was dated 1706 under the title *L'Innocente justifiée, histoire de Grenade par Mademoiselle de la Rocheguilhen, auteur de l'histoire des favorites divisée en trois parties suivant la copie.*   Compared to other novels by Mlle de la Roche-Guilhen, the above-mentioned work is rather long.   It contains 425 pages, while her other works are composed of less than 200 pages each.   It tells the story of the war between two clans: the Abencerages and the Zégris.   There are many closely related tales in it, but the main story is about Zaraïde and her liberator, Almanzor.   The young hero saves Zaraïde several times, but most importantly, he comes to her rescue when she is unjustly accused of adultery—hence the title of this novel.   Zaraïde soon discovers that Almanzor is actually Ponce de Leon, a Spanish knight disguised as a Moor.   After Grenada has been invaded and captured by the Spanish, Zaraïde becomes a Christian, under the name Isabella de Grenade, and finally marries Ponce de Leon.

Les amours de Néron was first published in 1695, but Anne de la Roche-Guilhen's name does not appear in it until the second edition is printed in 1713.   In this novel, Néron, the main character, shows no regard whatsoever for faithfulness in marriage. He is actually in love with Actée, a captive.

Having appeared in eight editions, *Histoire des favorites* seems to have been la Roche-Guilhen's most successful work.   This collection of short stories (or novelettes) was first published in 1697.   Many of the publications were identical except for minor changes; however, two short stories were added in the 1703 edition, and in the 1714 edition many short stories were included that were apparently not written by la Roche-Guilhen (Calame 59).

Histoire des favorites tells the story of the many grievances of women (whose names appear in the titles of the short stories) who were all connected in some way with kings, princes, and other men who held high positions in society. In one particular case, in the *Histoire de Julie de Farnèse*, a Pope falls in love with Julie de Farnèse and makes her brother a cardinal and his confidant. However, Julie marries another. Seeking vengeance, the Pope prepares a poisoned bottle of wine for the cardinal, Julie's brother. Unaware of his impending doom, the Pope drinks the wine himself and dies.

According to the *Dictionnaire des romans* (Delcro 851), the first edition of Anne de la Roche-Guilhen's *Amitié singulière* was published in 1700. Nevertheless, a copy which appeared in 1710 is identified as the third edition; this means that two others preceded it. This novel was also published in the *Histoires tragiques et galantes* in 1715 and again in 1723. The action takes place in Mexico. When the queen discovers that her friend is in love with her husband, the king of "Montezume," she decides to share both husband and throne with her.

La Nouvelle Talestris was published in 1700, and it was re-edited in 1721 and 1735. The first part of the novel is about the people in "Caux" who amused themselves by telling stories about their lives (and especially about their love affairs). The second part tells the story of a young girl who has been driven insane by reading la Calprenède's novel, *Cassandre* (5,483 pages). Possibly, la Roche-Guilhen had read it herself and found it to be mind-boggling.

Another attribution to la Roche-Guilhen, *Sapho*, appeared in 1706. This work contains two short stories: *Sapho ou l'heureuse inconstance* and *Le jeune Alcée ou la vertu triomphante*. The former takes place in Lesbos where Sappho, a female poet, falls in love with Phaon, who is in love with Sapho's best friend. However, Sapho no longer wants Phaon; she leaves Lesbos and marries another. Alcée ou la vertu triomphante is a continuation of the first short story, for it tells the story of the next generation.

The young Alcée, the son of Alcée and Sapho's friend, is in love with Cleis, Sapho's daughter. Even though Sapho's husband is against their union, and in spite of all the many obstacles, the young Alcée and Cleis find happiness together.

Jacqueline de Bavière was published in 1707. It is not clear that this was indeed the first edition, but the 1707 edition was followed by one in 1710, 1715, 1742, 1749, 1758, 1761? and in 1785. *Jacqueline de Bavière* is a fairly accurate historical account of the life of a princess who lived during the fifteenth century. The heroine is forced to marry le duc de Brabant for political reasons. Jacqueline soon runs away and marries another. However, le duc de Brabant has the second marriage annulled.

During the same year (1707), another of Anne de la Roche-Guilhen's works, *Dernières Oeuvres*, was published. This collection of short stories appeared again in 1708 and 1709, with the title *Histoire curieuses et galantes*. *Elizabeth d'Angoulême*, the first of the five short stories included in this work, tells the story of a beautiful princess who has many admirers (including the king, Hugues, who plans to marry her), and who is kidnapped the night before her wedding by Jean, the king of England. She is forced to marry Jean. It is only after his death that Elizabeth, the princess, is free to find happiness with Hugues, the king of France.

The second short story is entitled *Adelaïde, Reine de Hongrie*. Adelaïde is married to Ladislas, the king of Hungary, but Wenceslas, the king's brother, falls in love with Adelaïde, who rebukes him. Thus, Wenceslas tells the king that his wife Adelaïde has been unfaithful to him. The king gives the order to have Adelaïde stabbed to death. Deeply saddened by the news of Adelaide's death, Wenceslas confesses that he lied. Ladislas then discovers that the queen had not been killed as he had ordered and asks for her forgiveness.

The third story, *Agrippine*, takes place in Rome. It tells the story of Tibère, the son of Livie, who kidnaps Agrippine the night before she was to be married to Asinius Gallus. The Emperor is angered and plans to ban Tibère from the court. Fortunately,

Livie obtains his forgiveness.

Thémir ou Tamerlan, the fourth short story, was later published in *Oeuvres de Mme de Villedieu* in 1712 under the title *Tamerlan et Orixène*. It begins with a history of two rival families. The action centers around the conflict between the sons, who are both in love with Orixène, the princess of Tartarie. Orixène openly reveals her preference for Armetzar over Calix. The families then engage in a physical battle. Armetzar's father wins the war but dies from wounds received in battle. Armetzar is then forced to leave and find a home elsewhere. However, with the help of a friend, he returns to free Orixène from her captors. At last, Armetzar and Orixène find happiness together.

The last short story included in the *Dernières Oeuvres*, *Hiéron, Roi de Syracuse*, tells the story of Hiéron, who is envied and hated by many. Appius Claudius, the king of Carthage, attacks Sicily many times but is always turned back by the invincible Hiéron. Soon, Hiéron decides to put an end to these attempts by invading and conquering the country of the Carthaginians. Nevertheless, while away, serving his country in battle, he nearly loses his beloved Artemire.

Another novel attributed to Anne de la Roche-Guilhen, *La Foire de Beaucaire*, as the author explains in the preface, is a novel about men instead of princesses. The action takes place in an inn during the fair of Beaucaire. Two men meet, and each tells the other about his romantic adventures. There are problems in both affairs, but they each have a happy ending.

The last work that has been accredited to our author, *Oeuvres diverses*, is another collection of short stories. It was published in 1711, four years after the death of Anne de la Roche-Guilhen. The first short story is entitled *Atilla, Roi des Huns*. It is the story of a very cruel king named Atilla; the mere mentioning of his name incites fear in everyone. Atilla receives a beautiful princess, Honorie, as a peace offering. She joins Atilla's many other wives and mistresses. Being a new arrival, Honorie tells her life's story to the others and then listens as they tell their stories to her.

The second short story in *Oeuvres diverses* is called *Histoire d'Axiane*. Axiane, a princess, is being held captive, and Polémir, a valiant soldier who is in love with her, is searching for Axiane. When he arrives where Axiane is being held prisoner, he tells the story to a soldier in the army of his enemy. It appears that this short story was never finished; it ends once Polémir has finished his story. The reader never learns what happened after Polémir's arrival.

The third short story is entitled *Sigismond, Roi de Pologne*. The king of *Pologne* is told that he will have a son who will cause the death of his mother, dethrone him, and require his father's life. The queen actually has a son and dies giving birth to him. The child is given the name Sigismond. Frightened by what has happened, the king puts him in a dungeon where he is to remain forever. Finally, the king can no longer bear to keep his son imprisoned, so he lets Sigismond out and tells him that he is his father. Sigismond goes into a rage, threatens to kill his father and is forced to return to the dungeon. When the citizens of *Pologne* find out what the king has done, they invade the castle and set Sigismond free. Ultimately, the king decides to give the throne to Sigismond.

Anne de la Roche-Guilhen's novels are certainly not lacking in romance or adventure. La Roche-Guilhen surrounds her heroines with many suitors who often kidnap, fight, or even kill in order to have their beloved all to themselves. The heroes are so obsessed with the idea of finding eternal bliss with the heroines that they often risk their lives for their beloved. Frequently in la Roche-Guilhen's novels, we find brothers attempting to kill brothers, and fathers plotting to kill sons. In many instances, the hero finds himself travelling abroad, fighting villains who dared to kidnap his beloved princess. Sometimes the hero tries to conquer the passion he feels by running away, but he inevitably returns. Although la Roche-Guilhen's works are similar in that they all dramatize the love relationship of the heroes and heroines, the novelistic techniques she employs are quite varied and skillful.

Chapter Two

Plot: A "Technique" Device in the Works of Anne de la Roche-Guilhen

Plot, a systematic procedure in literary works, has enjoyed a varied existence. It has not, however, attracted the attention of many modern critics who are invariably more interested in treating themes (love, revenge, etc.), narrative technique, characterization or psychological aspects. Nevertheless, plot is an integral part of literary compositions such as novels and plays, and it is oftentimes the controlling factor in writing. The type of narration and characters used in a novel, in many cases, depends largely upon the plot. The plot is the total result of what the author has attempted to say and it is therefore the plot that determines whether the writer has effectively accomplished his goal. In *Technique in Fiction*, Macauley and Lanning explain that

> . . . plot is an artifice. It arouses and directs the reader's expectations. It has the sense of predestination. It imposes a unity on the narration so that all of the happenings interrelate, in the end, to make a whole. (158)

Elements of Plot

Plot is often defined in terms of its relation to story. Most critics tend to agree that story is basically " . . . a narrative of events arranged in their time sequence" (E. M. Forster 221). A plot, then, is no more than a story with the addition of an explanation of the cause of the events. Macauley and Lanning define plot as:

> . . . a pattern of cause and effect. One event forces another to occur or one happening causes something hitherto withheld to be revealed. It is only at the end, when the events have reached culmination, that the pattern is complete. (159)

In his *Aspects of the Novel*, Forster gives a simple, but practical illustration of story and plot. Forster's example of story is: "The king died, and the queen died" (221). Clearly there are two events in this story, one succeeding the other. There is apparently more to the story than what is given in this sentence, however. The author or storyteller may choose to give some information about the character of the king and queen or something may be said about their daily lives. Nevertheless, once the cause of either of these events is given, the story becomes a plot. Forster used the same two events to illustrate plot: "The king died, and then the queen died of grief" (221). Thus the cause (of the death of the queen) is the death of the king and the effect (of the death of the king) is the death of the queen.

Although the subject matter may vary, all plots are related in some way to time since cause and effect must take place in time. Oftentimes, the story is told in the order in which the events took place. However, the author or storyteller sometimes interrupts this narrative pattern to take a look back into the past. This technique is called the flashback. In this study, the term flashback is used in its traditional and literal sense; it is a narrative device in which the normal chronological order of the action is interrupted by the author (or narrator) in order to relate an earlier event. Flashback is not treated here in the modern sense: when an action, a thought, even a smell or taste trigger a synesthetic reaction whereby a past and forgotten event suddenly surfaces at the conscious level. As Majorie Boulton explains, "The flashback is common: some of the story is related in the obvious time sequence, but part is narrated by one of the characters, or in some document or letter, and this explains what has gone before" (63). Thus the flashback may be realized in several ways (a document, a letter, etc.), but it is used to show what has transpired before the time that it appears or even before the beginning of the narration of the events. It is quite useful in explaining how a character came to find himself in a particular situation, giving information about the past life of the character and showing what happened in a location other than that where the story is being told.

The *deus ex machina* is another element of plot. It is a device designed to set characters free from unconquerable dilemmas. Some of the great ancient writers, such as Euripides, saved their characters by allowing one of the gods to descend and deliver them. In a play, a machine was used to represent the particular god and it was literally lowered onto the stage. This machine-god was also used in the plays of some seventeenth-century playwrights (Rotrou's play *Iphigénie* for example). However, in modern works (plays and novels), it has taken on a new form:

> In somewhat more modern drama, he [*deus ex machina*] takes on the form of the rich uncle or whatever; he is from India, or wherever; and he forgives Clarence, reunites him with Arabella, and provides a liberal cash settlement. (Macauley and Lanning 163)

Thus, cause and effect, flashback and the *deus ex machina* are all elements of plot and are used in this chapter's examination of plot in three of Anne de la Roche-Guilhen's novels: *Almanzaïde*, *Le Grand Scanderberg*, and *Zingis*. Of the three elements mentioned above, cause and effect is the most prevalent in the works of our author. This, nevertheless is not unusual, for if any novel (by any author) has a plot (Most novels do have a plot whether it be a plot of action, of character or of thought.), inevitably there is an abundance of cause and effect.

Although this chapter focuses on cause and effect, the flash-back, and the *deus ex machina*, as they relate to the works of Anne de la Roche-Guilhen, we must point out that cause and effect and the flashback are equally characteristic of the novels of other seventeenth-century writers such as Mme de Villedieu, Madeleine de Scudéry and Mme de La Fayette. However, la Roche-Guilhen introduces in the narrative of the seventeenth-century a third element—the *deus ex machina*—to rescue her characters from the tragic perils of love.

Cause and Effect

In *Almanzaïde*, *Le Grand Scanderberg* and *Zingis*, the main theme of cause and effect, which invariably leads to trouble, is love. The hero, in each case, is in love with some beautiful princess who for one reason or another is never in a position to return his love. Love is a powerful force in the novels of Mademoiselle de la Roche-Guilhen. In the preface of *Le Grand Scanderberg*, she defends the fact that her heroes are in love by writing a long exposé on the subject, referring to history for support:

> Peut-être auroit-on de la peine à trouver un seul homme raisonnable qui n'ait point aimé. Les plus grands Héros même n'ont pû s'en défendre. . . . Alexandre & César qui commandoient à prés de la moitié du monde, faisoient gloire d'obéir au sexe qui en a toujours fait plus belle partie. Hercule, ce prodige de force & de valeur, préféra de porter des chaines d'une femme, à l'honneur de porter le ciel & les Dieux . . . Mars même, le Dieu de la Guerre, ne pût résister aux attraits de la Déesse des Grâces & des Amours; & il se croyoit trop heureux de partager avec Vulcain les faveurs de Vénus. (la Roche-Guilhen 3-4).

Great men such as Caesar, strong men like Hercules and even the gods were unable to resist the power of love. Likewise, the heroes of Anne de la Roche-Guilhen are completely overwhelmed by this powerful adversary—love. Love-passion in la Roche-Guilhen is intensified by the fact that the author's Huguenot spiritual background echoes the Pascalian Jansenistic theme of fate, hence an inherent devouring force that dominates the character. Love is the main cause of suffering for the character, for his inner anguish is the result of the hero's inability to overcome this powerful passion, thus showing the weakness of man when faced with uncontrollable forces.

In *Almanzaïde*, the jealousy of Roxane, the wife of the king, causes her to commit many malicious acts. She has great plans for her son and would go to any length to see to it that he alone is the king's sole heir. Roxane even attempts to poison Cleonis who is also one of the king's wives:

> Comme les incommoditez de la grossesse de Cleonis lui ôtoit le goust des viandes, elle s'en plaignit un iour chez Roxane, qui fit apporter des corbeilles de fruits admirables, dont elle mangea avec plaisir . . . Mais elle se fut à peine retirée à son appartement, qu'elle tomba dans un mal dont la violence fit d'abord désespérer de sa vie; je [Aristan is speaking to Almanzor] la [Cleonis] trouvay entre les bras de ses Esclaves sans couleur, & presque sans mouvement. (80-81)

Though the main cause of this cruel act on the part of Roxane is jealousy—she (Roxane) did not like the fact that Cleonis had captured the king's heart—she was also afraid that Cleonis would replace her by gaining complete control over King Abdala. Fortunately, it is realized in time that Cleonis has been poisoned; thus with the proper treatment, she gets well. However, the effect of Roxane's jealousy does not end there; it is also Roxane's jealousy that causes Cleonis to pretend that her baby, Almanzor, was stillborn. It is decided that the time of the birth would be hidden from Roxane, and the child would be taken from the palace and placed in the care of others:

Cleonis conceut mes raisons [Aristan is speaking to Alman-
zor], le Roy vint, nous prîmes nos mesures, & celles qui
nous parurent les plus seures, ce fut de cacher le temps de
l'accouchement de Cleonis, afin de feindre vostre mort.
Cela réussit heureusement, vous vinstes au monde; ie vous
mis hors du Palais entre les main de personnes que j'avois
pratiquées, & qui m'étoient fidelles. (86-87)

Another cause and effect situation found in *Almanzaïde* is the
return of Almanzor and his sister Almanzaïde to the palace. After
several years had passed, it was thought that it was safe to bring
the children home, but only if they were disguised. Thus,
Almanzor, six years after his birth, was brought back to the palace
and given to the king as a slave: "Six ans s'écoulèrent après
lesquels ie crus que ie ne hazarderois rien à vous faire entrer dans
ce Palais. Un marchand supposé vous donna à Abdala comme
Esclave . . ." (91). Almanzaïde was returned to the palace two
years later and was given to Roxane with the hope that Roxane
would grow to love her. So Almanzor and Almanzaïde, who
unknowingly are the king's own flesh and blood, find themselves
living in the palace, yet unable to fully enjoy the royal riches that
are rightfully theirs. Nevertheless, they are both able to rise above
their predicament and find favor with the king as well as with
Roxane. Almanzor, by his own merit, becomes one of the king's
favorite subjects. Almanzaïde is not treated maliciously by
Roxane; she is therefore able to live happily.

The return of Almanzor and Almanzaïde to the palace is the
cause of contrasting effects. Although they both must live as
servants, only Almanzor finds some form of contentment. On the
other hand, Almanzaïde repeatedly expresses her dissatisfaction.
These expressions of uneasiness eliminate an element of mystery
concerning Almanzaïde's birth; they convince the reader that it is
possible that she is indeed a princess. Nevertheless, in this event
of cause and effect, emphasis is placed on the struggle of the
characters.

Another effect of their return to the palace is that Almanzor and Almanzaïde fall in love—not cognizant of their brother-sister relationship. Even during their youth, Almanzaïde had already captured Almanzor's heart. He loved to be in her presence; when he was not with her, he was always depressed. He used every opportunity to see her. The love that Almanzor has for Almanzaïde even causes him to neglect his studies. The reader discovers this effect of love when Almanzor makes a confession to Aristan: " . . . ie vous confesse mesme que ie mumurois quand vous m'occupiez à des leçons trop longues, dont ie ne pensois qu'à elle [Almanzaïde]" (25-26).

During his young adult years, Almanzor becomes very melancholic because Almanzaïde has been promised to another. The king has promised his wife Roxane that he would give Almanzaïde to her son, Abdemar, as a wife. This promise seems to be a detrimental blow to any hope that Almanzor would have Almanzaïde as his own. Thus he becomes even more discouraged. Nevertheless, after the death of Roxane and Abdemar, it appears that there is nothing that could possibly stand in the way of Almanzor's and Almanzaïde's happiness. It is at this point however that Aristan decides to reveal a horrible secret: Almanzor and Almanzaïde are sister and brother. The young lovers are so devastated that they both, in search of solitude as well as a means of extinguishing their fiery passion, take to their respective rooms for three days:

Il [Almanzor] fut trois iours sans sortir de sa chambre, & Almanzaïde garda le lit pendant le mesme temps, pour cacher un trouble dont elle n'étoit pas maistresse; elle craignoit de revoir un frère qu'elle aimoit avec trop d'ardeur, & ce misérable Prince craignant aussi de confondre toujours sa soeur & son Amante, n'avoit pas la force d'aller chez Roxane, quoy qu'il y fust porté par les mesme empressemens. (99-100)

Consequently, the disclosure of Aristan's secret causes la Roche-Guilhen's hero and heroine to become trapped in a state of catatonia; prisoners, they are physically unable to leave their respective rooms and incapable of lucidly considering their situation and deciding how they should proceed with their lives. They do realize however that seeing each other would only escalate their torment.

At one point in the plot of *Almanzaïde*, Cleonis decides to write a note and send it to Almanzor asking him to meet her secretly. It is her intention to try to help resolve the dilemma he is in (He was in love with a person he could not have as his own.). As stated by the narrator, "Que cet innocent Billet causa du trouble dans le Palais d'Abdala . . ." (146), this note causes complete chaos in the palace. While the slave is on his way to deliver the note, Roxane sees it. Roxane takes the note, reads it, and concludes that Cleonis and Almanzor are having an affair. The next day, Roxane tells the king of her suspicions. The king does not believe her until he reads the note himself. He swears vengeance. The king is furious that the man he admired most has betrayed him; he is further infuriated because the wife he loves most is taking part in this betrayal. He is so troubled that he is unable to sleep that night. Consequently, he gives the order to have both Almanzor and Cleonis killed: "Enfin, l'irrité Abdala ne voulut plus différer sa vangeance, & le soir de ce mesme iour, des bourreaux destinez aux executions secrettes, eurent ordre d'aller priver de la vie Cleonis & Almanzor" (162).

Having discovered that the king has given the order to have Almanzor and Cleonis killed, Almanzaïde goes to the king and informs him that she and Almanzor are his daughter and son and that Cleonis is their mother. She also tells him that their identity has been kept secret to protect them (Almanzor and Almanzaïde) from the vicious Roxane. The king sends his stepson, Abdemar, to stop the execution of Almanzor and Cleonis. Abdemar soon returns with the news that he arrived in time to save the life of Cleonis but too late to save that of Almanzor (It is later discovered that it was not Almanzor who had been killed, but Taxare, the slave who allowed Roxane to take the note.

All of the cause and effect events in *Zingis* are clearly connected to the hero's uncontrollable passion. Once he has met his beloved, she becomes the center of his life. Thereafter, he devotes all of his efforts to pleasing her. Zingis' struggle begins as soon as he meets his beloved Taxila: he must fight his jealous rival, Timur. As the cause and effect events proceed to unfold, Zingis saves his beloved's life; fights a war with the king, his beloved's father; attacks and nearly kills his rival; goes into hiding; attempts to rescue his beloved from the palace; is arrested and sentenced to be executed; escapes and kills his rival.

Zingis opens with the enamored Zingis outside the palace trying to break in to rescue his beloved mistress, Taxila. He is discovered however and arrested. The king, Undkan, is totally controlled by his evil wife, Zamar who has persuaded him to give his daughter to her son, Timur, in marriage. Zingis has informed the king that he wants Taxila as his own wife, but his wishes are ignored. Thus Zingis' love for Taxila causes him to try to kidnap his beloved. As a result of his thoughtless behavior, Zingis, a young man who is admired by everyone, finds himself in a life-threatening predicament. King Undkan, influenced by his wife, decides to execute Zingis. Love is certainly the main source of motivation in this, the first cause and effect event in *Zingis*. Emphasis is placed upon the overwhelming effect love has on the characters; but more importantly, the above event evokes the reader's curiosity.

In *Zingis*, even the hero's reputation for bravery becomes an element of cause and effect. As a result of Zingis' many valiant feats as a warrior, many of the kings of neighboring countries come to congratulate Undkan for having captured him. Most of these royal leaders are happy to know that Zingis is a prisoner and that he will soon die. However, there are two of them who feel that Zingis has been wrongfully imprisoned. Thus, they join forces and make plans to free him. One of these kings is Zingis' friend Almundzar. After learning that Philing, another of the kings, admires Zingis, Almundzar has one of his servants tell him the life story of Zingis. Philing then decides to help Almundzar free Zingis.

The above-mentioned cause and effect events inform the reader that Zingis will not be left in limbo forever. His way of escape, which is directly related to his renown, is arranged by way of the union of two kings who are among those who assemble at the king's palace. Furthermore, these same cause and effect events reveal information previously withheld. Since one of the kings who agree to rescue Zingis knows nothing about Zingis's personal life, he must hear Zingis' story, which explains how Zingis was captured by Undkan.

While Zerbin, Almundzar's servant, is telling Philing the story of Zingis' life, the reader learns how Zingis happened to meet and fall in love with Taxila. After traveling into distant countries, fighting battles to make a name for himself, Zingis finally decides to return home. On his way home, he discovers that his father has gone to another city. So, he goes there in search of his father. Tired from his trip, he enters one of the beautiful gardens of the palace where he meets several beautiful princesses. Taxila is among them. When Zingis sees Taxila, he immediately falls in love with her. However, many obstacles present themselves, causing Zingis to have to fight a new battle.

As soon as he sees and falls in love with Taxila, Zingis finds himself confronted with his first obstacle. Timur surprises him and attempts to chase him from the garden. Nevertheless, Timur is no match for Zingis; Zingis wounds him. The king arrives, assesses the situation, finds Zingis blameless and invites him to stay. Furthermore, king Undkan honors Zingis with many lavish luxuries.

Thus a virtual war develops between Zingis and Timur for Taxila's love and attention. After deciding to give Taxila a big party on her birthday, Timur arranges for many activities, one of which is a boat ride for everybody. The boat in which Taxila is riding overturns, and Taxila nearly drowns. Timur panics and begins yelling for one of his soldiers to save her. In the meantime, Zingis sees what has happened, jumps into the river and saves Taxila who is very grateful; she now begins to hate Timur, for he is a coward who was not willing to risk his life to save hers. Thus, Timur's attempt to express his love for Taxila (by giving a party in her honor) is indirectly the cause of her hate for him.

As a result of the above incident, Timur's mother the queen, Zamar, expresses her joy that Taxila was saved and tells her that she would have gladly risked her life to save her. Smiling, Taxila replies that, if the queen's statement is true, she would have done more than many men:

> . . . & se rencontrant dans une galerie commune, Madame, dit Zamar à la Princesse [Taxila], je loüe le Ciel du soin qu'il a pris de vos jours, & je vous assure, que dans le moment où je vis vôtre vie exposée, j'aurois de bon coeur hazardé la mienne pour vous conserver. Vous auriez beaucoup plus fait, Madame, repliqua Taxila en soûriant modestement, que beaucoup d'hommes n'ont pu faire, & vous voyez que dans le sein des Etats du Roi mon Père, il ne s'est trouvé que deux Princes étrangers assez généreux pour mépriser le peril . . . (la Roche-Guilhen 32)

Even Zamar recognizes that Taxila clearly loves Zingis and hates Timur: "Zamar vit bien dans ce discours la reconoissance de Taxila pour Zingis, & son mépris pour Timur . . ." (33).

Zamar devotes all of her efforts toward pleasing and establishing a lucrative inheritance for her son, Timur. She decides that Tartarie is not large enough and tells Undkan that he should require the neighboring countries to pay tribute to him:

> Dans ce temps là, Zamar, qui vouloit étendre les limites de la Tatarie dans l'esperence d'y voir regner son fils, fit comprendre à Undkan qu'il étoit honteux pour lui, avec tant de puissances, de ne pas exiger de ses voisins des tributs qu'il lui étoit aisé de leur imposer. (42-43)

This demand angers the kings of the neighboring countries, and they all refuse to pay tribute to Undkan. War is declared.

Undkan gives Timur an army to command, but Zingis fights along side Undkan. Zingis fights with valor, saving the king's life and capturing three kings. As a reward, Zingis is given the right to decide what should be done to them. He spares their lives once they promise to pay tribute to Undkan. Timur and his army, on the contrary, are chased by the king of Ung. Zingis and Undkan find Timur and bring him back to do battle. Finally they are victorious and return to Cambalu.

The news of what happened during the war spreads throughout the city. Again, Zingis has proved himself a great hero while Timur reveals his cowardice. Taxila's love for Zingis and hate for Timur grow. She is so disgusted with Timur, who brags of what he would have done had the situation been different, that she tells him that he should have been killed. Now, Timur is even more afraid that he will lose her to Zingis; so he goes to his mother and tells her that Taxila loves Zingis. As usual, Zamar promises to solve the problem. She tells Undkan of Taxila's betrayal and finally persuades him to announce the wedding of Timur and Taxila.

The wedding announcement of Timur and Taxila is the first of a series of cause and effect events that follow. When Zingis discovers that Undkan plans to announce the wedding, he goes into a rage and decides to kill Timur. He attacks Timur and wounds him badly. His friend Almundzar takes Zingis into hiding in a nearby forest. He encourages Zingis to leave the country, but he refuses to do so before seeing and talking to Taxila. A secret meeting is arranged. Taxila tells him that he must leave the country. Zingis submits to her wishes. He returns to his native land and begins training an army to fight Undkan in case he attacks. Undkan does not attack. Zingis becomes restless, so he sends a band of soldiers to ask Undkan to send Taxila to him. Undkan refuses. In the meantime, Zingis fights many battles and adds a lot of territory to his kingdom. Soon he makes plans to kidnap Taxila. It is during his attempt to do so that Zingis is captured and becomes Undkan's prisoner.

Finally, the day of Zingis' public execution arrives. When the executioner is about to kill Zingis, his soldiers, led by Philing and Almundzar, attack. Zingis and his soldiers quickly kill all of the adversaries who resist. Zamar tries to get others, including the kings, to attack, but no one is brave enough to do so. On the contrary, Undkan, followed by the other kings, runs into the palace. During the battle, Zingis notices a soldier who is about to kill Undkan; Zingis quickly instructs him to spare the king's life. Soon, another group of Undkan's soldiers arrive. Timur, noticing the great number of soldiers, decides to lead them in battle. Zingis kills Timur. Zamar, watching from a window, falls and goes into convulsions. Two hours later, it is announced that she has died, having witnessed her son's murder. It is Timur's cowardice and haughtiness that cause his death; it is Zamar's love for her son that causes her death.

At the moment Zingis' executioner is about to kill him, the fact that cause and effect is closely related to time becomes apparent. The reader has already been informed of the plan to set Zingis free; therefore, his curiosity is aroused. The reader, like la Roche-Guilhen's characters, is not left in limbo. Immediately, Zingis' soldiers attack, and a series of cause and effect events begin to unfold. The attack is the initial and main cause of the chain of events that follow. This attack is the direct cause of the death of many of Zingis' enemies, including Timur. Because Zamar watches her son die, she succumbs to the same fate. Within the brief period of time it takes these events to unfold, Zingis is totally delivered: he has been rescued from prison; and he is now free to find happiness with his beloved Taxila.

The treatment of cause and effect in *Le Grand Scanderberg* is quite different from that found in *Zingis*. While the cause and effect events in Zingis deal with the hero's worthiness in battle, the ones in *Le Grand Scanderberg* emphasize Scanderberg's sadness and weakness. The first cause and effect event is quite unique, for it is presented in reverse order. As the plot begins to unfold, the reader experiences the effect of some unknown cause. The effect is Scanderberg's extreme sadness. The cause is revealed only after Scanderberg has thoroughly lamented, and his friend has begged him to share his secret.

Scanderberg would sometimes seek solitude because of his inability to have Arianisse as his own. One day, he goes off with Urane, his companion, to whom he finally admits that love is the cause of his sadness. Suddenly, they hear a voice crying out for help. They rush to offer assistance and find that it is the eunuch who took care of Scanderberg during his youth, Aradin, who is badly wounded and dies before he is able to explain what has happened to him. While Scanderberg grieves and complains aloud about Aradin's demise, Urane checks Aradin's body to make sure he is dead. While doing so, he discovers a letter. The letter is an order from the king, Amurat, telling Orcan to kill Arianisse because she refuses to respond to Amurat's advances. Concluding that Arianisse is already dead, Scanderberg is more grievous than ever. He declares openly that he would gladly give his life to avenge her death.

In the meantime, Thopia discovers that Scanderberg has left the palace without a military escort; he, along with an army, sets out to find Scanderberg. They all return to the palace where Thopia promises to help Scanderberg avenge Arianisse's death once he has heard how Scanderberg came to fall in love with Arianisse. Thus, Scanderberg begins to tell his story. He tells Thopia that Amurat was such a powerful king that all of Asia feared him. Scanderberg's father, a king himself, was so afraid of Amurat that he gave Scanderberg and his three brothers to him as a peace offering. Amurat grows very fond of Scanderberg. He begins to treat him as a son, leaving his three brothers in slavery. Scanderberg becomes such a great warrior that Amurat makes him the commander of five thousand soldiers in spite of Scanderberg's youthfulness—only nineteen years old.

When Scanderberg finally meets Arianisse who is one of Amurat's slaves, he is completely captivated by her beauty. He does not, however, make his emotions known to her at first. Instead, he admires her from a distance for quite some time. One day while he is sitting on the bank of a river, he notices a woman in the water drowning. Immediately, he jumps in to save her.

When he gets her back to the bank, he realizes it is Arianisse. When she regains consciousness, he admits to her that he loves her. She tells him, however, that she is not worthy of him.

Scanderberg soon discovers that he has two rivals. They are none other than the emperor himself, Amurat, and Mahamet. Scanderberg feels so threatened by his rivals that he writes a note to Arianisse to tell her how much he loves her. He sends it to her by a trusted friend. Arianisse does not want to accept the letter because she thinks it is a ploy instituted by her captor, Amurat, to find out if she is unfaithful. She reads it and instructs the messenger to tell Scanderberg to forget about her.

Nevertheless, one day Arianisse decides to go into the garden to think about her predicament. She speaks out loud about her love for Scanderberg and dislike for the emperor, Amurat. She does not know that her three suitors are listening. Unfortunately, the king soon discovers the other men and promises Scanderberg that he shall die for having betrayed him. Amurat has Scanderberg put in prison and Arianisse locked in her room with guards at the door. One of Scanderberg's friends convinces Arianisse to write a letter to Scanderberg. Although she does not admit it openly in the letter, Scanderberg is assured that she loves him. Upon learning of Scanderberg's imprisonment, the people begin to protest. Thus, Amurat decides to free Scanderberg. Before leaving the country as planned, however, Scanderberg is allowed the satisfaction of seeing Arianisse.

One particular cause and effect event in *Le Grand Scanderberg* is designed solely to display Scanderberg's passion for Arianisse. It does not advance the action; and it is not related to any other event of cause and effect. While the fire, which threatens Arianisse's life, is the cause, Scanderberg's willingness to risk his life is the effect. This incident takes place one night when the building in which Arianisse is held captive bursts into flames; everyone tries to extinguish the fire, but Arianisse and others would have perished had it not been for Scanderberg, who is brave enough to walk on hot coals in order to rescue them: "Je [Scanderberg] marchai sur des morceaux de cendres brûlantes jusques à une galerie, où les femmes & plusieurs Eunuques attendoient leur dernier malheur . . . je courus à Arianisse . . ." (83). Arianisse is deeply touched that Scanderberg has saved her life a second time.

Thus, being exiled from the ones he loves and having read the letter from Amurat giving Orcan the order to kill Arianisse, Scanderberg decides to declare war against Amurat. In the meantime, Scanderberg discovers that Arianisse is alive. For the first time, Scanderberg is very happy: "La joye de Scanderberg fut alors des plus grandes" (97).

Meanwhile, Amurat goes to Arianisse's father to try to get him to convince her to return his love. Her father refuses to cooperate. Amurat then threatens to kill her father if Arianisse does not reciprocate his love. Arianisse declares that she would rather see her father dead than give in to Amurat. Plans are made for the execution of Aranit, Arianisse's father. On the day the execution is to take place, Scanderberg arrives with his army just in time to save Aranit's life. Nevertheless, in the midst of the great battle, Musulman, another of Arianisse's admirers, kidnaps her. Musulman does everything within his power to get her to respond to his love, but she refuses to love him. Finally, Musulman is so enraged at Arianisse's persistent resistance that he threatens to kill her if she does not give in to his romantic advances. Scanderberg and Thopia, who have been chasing Musulman, arrive. Thopia goes quickly to Arianisse's rescue; he kills Musulman.

As the cause and effect events in *Le Grand Scanderberg* proceed to culminate, the desperation of the characters involved becomes visible. In despair, king Amurat goes to Arianisse's father in order to get him to persuade his daughter to return his love. Because the father refuses to give his assistance, Amurat goes to Arianisse again, threatening to kill her father if she continues to reject him. Amurat is rejected again; therefore, he makes plans to execute Arianisse's father as promised. Upon hearing that Arianisse's father's execution has been planned, Scanderberg is forced to return from exile to rescue him.

All of the cause and effect incidents found in *Almanzaïde*,

Zingis and *Le Grand Scanderberg* are not mentioned above; however, an attempt has been made to explore the most important ones. It is quite apparent that in each case, love is the main cause of most of the effects. The main hero is in love with a beautiful princess who is otherwise obligated. Being madly in love with this princess, the hero is dominated by his passion, thus making himself the victim of an apparent inevitable course of events against which he is powerless. Though he might ultimately succeed in overcoming many obstacles, la Roche-Guilhen's hero reveals an inner conflict not evident in other novelists of the century. For this reason, and perhaps due to her spiritual background[1], from which her hero's inner conflicts seem to spring, la Roche-Guilhen saves the hero from eternal doom by skillfully handling the *deus ex machina* technique.

Flashback

The flashbacks in *Almanzaïde, Zingis* and *Le Grand Scanderberg* appear most often in the form of a story told by one character to another. Actually, there is very little true action, in the literal sense of the word, in Anne de la Roche-Guilhen's novels. Some character is always telling another what has transpired in the past in order to explain how he came to be in his present predicament. The hero is usually in love with a lovely young woman who is unable to return his love; thus, we often find him in an extremely melancholic state at the outset. Invariably, a friend becomes concerned about his unhappiness and inquires as to its cause. The hero never refuses to share his troubles with a friend.

As the plot of *Almanzaïde* begins to unfold, we find Almanzor in a melancholic state of mind. One of the king's eunuchs, Aristan, who took care of Almanzor during his youth, recognizes his sadness and begs him to confide in him:

> . . . je n'ay point mérité que vous me fassiez un mystère de vos chagrins, ie vous vois dans une langeur qui vous accable, sans en pouvoir imaginer la cause . . . Parlez

donc, Almanzor, ie ne suis point indigne de vostre confi-
ance . . . (9-10)

Hesitating at first, Almanzor finally tells Aristan that he is in love
with Almanzaïde. Though Aristan tries to encourage him to forget
her and turn his attention toward someone else, Almanzor is
unable to do so. Furthermore, he admits that the real cause of his
sadness is his rival, Abdemar. After concluding from the
expression on Aristan's face that the eunuch is interested in his
adventures, Almanzor sets out to explain how he and Almanzaïde
met and how he fell in love with her. This flashback is given the
title: "Histoire d'Almanzor et d'Almanzaïde."

While telling his story, Almanzor sheds some light on the
character of Almanzaïde—she is virtuous and generous. He
explains that his feelings for her began during their youth, and that
Abdemar was destined to meet Almanzaïde, for she was his
mother's slave. Once he has met her, it becomes impossible to
resist falling in love with her. Abdemar tells Almanzaïde that he
loves her, but he soon discovers that she prefers Almanzor.
Abdemar has Almanzor banned from Almanzaïde's presence.

The second flashback in *Almanzaïde* is the story of the birth of
Almanzor and of Almanzaïde. Aristan tells this story to Almanzor
when he realizes how much Almanzor loves Almanzaïde. He
explains how the mother of Cleonis goes to the palace because she
is destitute. The king falls in love with Cleonis who becomes one
of the king's wives and gives birth to a son soon thereafter. In the
meantime, however, Roxane, another of the king's wives, becomes
very jealous of Cleonis because she has won the king's heart.
Thus Cleonis and her friends pretend that her first child, Almanzor, is stillborn. Aristan also explains that Cleonis gives birth to
another child, Almanzaïde, and the same ruse is employed again.
This flashback is a further complication of the main plot. Before
its appearance in the novel, Almanzor is aware of the fact that
Almanzaïde has been promised to Abdemar in marriage, but there
is still hope. Almanzor believed he was capable of overcoming
that obstacle, but now it is impossible to find happiness with

Almanzaïde who is apparently his sister.

The first flashback in *Le Grand Scanderberg* occurs when Scanderberg tells his life story to Thopia. He is only eight years old when he, his mother and brothers arrive in Amurat's palace. Scanderberg is reared according to Turkish customs. His name is changed from George to Scanderberg. Amurat, the king, sees to it that Scanderberg receives a good education. Amurat becomes very fond of Scanderberg; he refers to him as his right-hand man. One evening, Scanderberg hears the voice of a maiden singing; he falls in love with her. Finally he meets Arianisse and becomes even more captivated by her beauty. It is also by way of this flashback that the reader learns that Scanderberg saves the life of his beloved Arianisse on two separate occasions: he saves her from drowning and from a fire in her residence. This flashback also discloses Scanderberg's three rivals: Amurat, the king, Mahamet and Musulman. Once he discovers that Scanderberg is his rival, the king has him thrown into jail and has Arianisse locked in her room. Succinctly, it is by way of this flashback that we learn about Scanderberg's background. We discover how he happened to be in the court of Amurat, how he obtained favor with the king, how he falls in love with Arianisse and how he overcomes his three rivals.

After hearing Scanderberg's story, Thopia sets out to tell his own story to prove that his situation is as grave as that of Scanderberg, if not more so. Thopia begins by admitting that he is in love with Amisse, Scanderberg's sister. When Thopia was sixteen years old and Amisse thirteen, one day, while secretly watching her fish, he begins to sigh so loudly that she turns to him and accuses him of chasing the fish away. Thopia finally admits he is in love with her. At first she does not want to hear any talk about love, but when she sees that Thopia is very insistent, she tells him that she will return his love if he will be quiet and help her catch some fish. He obeys. They catch many fish and return to the palace. Amisse still refuses to return Thopia's love. Finally, the king gives Amisse to another warrior. Thopia confronts Balse, the young warrior to whom Amisse has been promised, and tells him

that he is in love with Amisse. Thopia also makes it clear to him
that he would die before he would allow Balse to marry Amisse.
A duel is planned to settle the matter. Thopia wounds Balse
badly, but when the king learns of what happened, he is furious
and declares that Thopia will be put to death if Balse dies. Balse
does indeed die. Thopia leaves the country in order to escape
death. However, he soon discovers that king Castriot is dead and
that Amurat has invaded and taken control of the country. Thopia
concludes his story, thus ending the second flashback which
informs the reader of Thopia's many struggles.

The first flashback in *Zingis* takes place when Zingis instructs
his trusted servant, Zerbin, to tell the story of Zingis and Taxila
to Philing, one of the kings who has come to congratulate king
Undkan for having captured the great Zingis. Zerbin begins by
explaining that Zingis is of royal birth and that he has one sister,
Zenelie, who was kidnapped when she was only three years old.
As a result, Zingis' mother dies. During his youth, Zingis wins
many battles; thus he becomes very famous in all of Europe and
Asia. When he returns home, he has to travel to a neighboring
country to see his father. Once Zingis has arrived in this foreign
land, he nearly kills Timur, falls in love with Taxila, proves to be
a valiant soldier in Undkan's army while saving Undkan's life and
capturing three kings, nearly kills Timur a second time (when he
learns that Undkan has announced the wedding date of Timur and
Taxila), and is forced to find refuge in another country. After
trying to distract himself by fighting wars and adding territory to
his kingdom, he finally realizes that he simply must see Taxila
again. Thus Zingis makes plans to secretly enter the palace to
kidnap Taxila. When he arrives at the gate, Zingis becomes
impatient and yells for someone to open it. Consequently, Zingis
is captured, put in prison and plans are made for his execution.
At this point, Zerbin ends the story of Zingis and Taxila.

While Almundzar, Zingis' good friend, is talking to Philing,
the latter decides to tell his story, which is given the title "Histoire
de Philing & d'Azione". This is the second flashback in *Zingis*.
Philing explains that he was only six years old when his father

died. One day, during his youth, Philing discovers Axione on the
bank of a river among the bloody bodies of several soldiers.
Immediately, he falls in love with her. Hildezar, the king, also
sees her and falls in love with her. The king plans to have Philing
marry his daughter, but Philing refuses to do so. Hildezar is
determined to get rid of Philing so that he may have Axione to
himself; so he starts a war and sends him off to fight, hoping he
would be killed. Philing returns victorious without having
received the least wound or having lost a single soldier. Nevertheless, Hildezar has kidnapped Axione. Philing goes after them and
finds Hildezar nearly dead. The latter explains that he has been
attacked and that Axione has been kidnapped from him. Hildezar
dies and Philing buries him. Philing then makes the acquaintance
of Undkan. Thus ends Philing's story.

Once all of the problems have been solved and everyone is free
to marry the one he loves, the reader may begin to anticipate the
end of the novel. However, yet another flashback, which seems to
have no real connection with the main plot—at least there is no
important connection, is encountered. The reader is told that the
other characters, those who have finally found true happiness,
insist that Omir tell his and Thamirise's story.

Omir begins his story by explaining that he is the son of a
conquered prince and that he was subjected to the king of Tartarie.
Undkan, the king, treats Omir like a son, but Timur, the king's
son, treats him like a slave. Omir runs away. He sees and falls
in love with Thamirise. She is locked in a certain section of the
palace where men are not allowed to enter. Thus, Omir dresses
like a woman so that he will be able to speak to her. He assumes
the name Irmise. He soon becomes the best friend of Thamirise.
He is deeply saddened when he finds out that Thamirise has two
other suitors. She asks him why he is so sad, and he admits that
he is in love with her. Nothing more is said about Omir's
confession until one day, Thamirise's two suitors arrive and try to
kidnap her. A fierce battle takes place and many soldiers are
killed. Omir draws a sword from the body of one of the dead
soldiers and begins to fight Thamirise's suitors. He is attacked

from behind and is badly wounded. Once he is carried into the palace to be cared for, it is discovered that he is a man. Thus the two suitors get together and decide to kill Omir, but Omir leaves with Thamirise to go to Cambalu. Omir adds that they arrived the day before. Thus ends Omir's story.

The flashback plays a rather important role in the development of the plots of Anne de la Roche-Guilhen. Since she, like many of her contemporaries, frequently began her novels *in medias res*, the flashback was quite often a necessity. Since these works were begun *in medias res*, the flashback afforded the author an opportunity to go back in time and explain what had happened before the beginning of the novel. *Almanzaïde*, *Le Grand Scanderberg* and *Zingis* all begin *in medias res*. *Almanzaïde* begins with eight pages of introduction, giving the reader pertinent information about the setting (in *Maroc*), and describing the character of king Abdala and his relationship to the other characters. The reader is also introduced to the hero and to his teacher and companion who happens to be one of the king's eunuchs. At the outset, the hero, Almanzor, is in a very sad state of mind. In order to explain the cause of Almanzor's melancholy, Mademoiselle de la Roche-Guilhen uses the flashback. It is only after Aristan, Almanzor's teacher and companion, begs him persistently (for five pages) that Almanzor reveals the cause of his sadness. Once Almanzor tells Aristan that he is in love with Almanzaïde, Almanzor proclaims " . . . l'émotion de vostre visage me marque déja l'interest que vous prenez à mes avantures" (20). Almanzor, after recognizing Aristan's desire to hear his story, begins to tell the "Histoire d'Almanzor et d'Almanzaïde".

In *Le Grand Scanderberg* the reader is given more information (than in *Almanzaïde*) before the appearance of the first flashback. One not only learns about the character of the great Scanderberg, but he is actually seen in action. After learning about the hero's rather frequent need to be alone, the reader is led into the action of the novel with " . . . sortant un matin avec le seul Urane [One of Scanderberg's servants], il prit le chemin d'un Valon qui plaisoit à sa melancolie" (7). On this particular day, Scanderberg chooses to find solitude, unknowingly, near the camp of his enemy. Urane tries to warn his master of the danger they are in, but Scanderberg asks him " . . . crois-tu que l'Armée d'Amurat me put faire trembler" (8)? They soon discover Aradin, Scanderberg's former teacher and companion, who is crying for help. He has been wounded and while trying to explain what has happened to him, he dies. Aradin does, however, manage to pronounce the names of Scanderberg's two enemies, Amurat and Musulman, and that of Scanderberg's beloved Arianisse before breathing his last breath. The mentioning of these names gives Scanderberg the impression that Arianisse is still alive.

Meanwhile, Urane checks the body to see if Aradin is really dead, and discovers a note. It is a letter from Amurat to his *grand visir*, Orcan, giving Orcan the order to kill Arianisse for having resisted Amurat's advances. After reading this letter, Scanderberg is ready to invade Amurat's camp single handedly and rescue his beloved Arianisse. Fortunately, Thopia, one of Scanderberg's princes, arrives. He, along with Urane, persuades Scanderberg to go back to the city (Croye) where he will be among friends. Thopia knew that Scanderberg was in love, but he did not know the details. Therefore, Thopia " . . . témoigna une forte envie d'en être informé." Of course Scanderberg is obliged to tell him every single detail. Hence the first flashback; the "Histoire de Scanderberg" requires seventy-five pages, nearly one third of the entire novel.

In *Zingis*, the action begins in the bedroom of the heroine, Zingis' beloved Taxila: "Une nuit que Taxila étoit occupée du souvenir de Zingis, elle entendit un grand bruit, & vit entrer le Roi son pere dans sa chambre . . ." (5). The king scolds her for having arranged a secret rendezvous with his worst enemy, Zingis, and commands his soldiers to keep her closely guarded in her room. He leaves abruptly. Taxila does not understand what has just happened, but one of the guards explains that Zingis has just tried to break into the palace to kidnap her. The evil queen, Zamar, heard him at one of the gates; she had him arrested, put in chains and thrown into a prison cell reserved for the worst of criminals.

Shortly after Taxila's discovery of what has happened to Zingis, the reader learns, by way of a flashback, how Zingis and Taxila first met and fell in love. Philing, one of the kings who came to congratulate Undkan for having captured the invincible Zingis, listens attentively while Zerbin tells him the "Histoire de Zingis & de la Princesse Taxila."

Clearly, in the works examined here, the flashback is used most often to take the reader back in time, explaining what has happened at another time or in another place. The flashback reveals what is hitherto withheld, and explains how a character happens to be in a particular situation. As indicated by its titles, the flashback is always the story of the character's life, and it is told by one character to another. It is more than a mere look back into the past, however, for it is the principal method of narration.

The Deus ex Machina

In the works of Anne de la Roche-Guilhen, the *deus ex machina* is usually some stranger who wanders into town bearing news that makes it possible for the hero to have the beautiful princess with whom he has fallen madly in love. This is especially true in *Almanzaïde*. When it seems that there is no hope, this modern *deus ex machina* appears from nowhere, and without performing any magic tricks, he declares that Almanzor and Almanzaïde are not sister and brother after all. He is the man to whom Aristan had entrusted Almanzaïde during her infancy in order to protect her from Roxane. The newly-arrived stranger admits that Almanzaïde died shortly after she was left in his care and that she was replaced with another infant, a princess from his country, who was also in danger of being killed. Almanzaïde has also become the heiress of the throne of her native country where she, after the wedding, reigns with Almanzor, her husband.

In *Zingis*, the *deus ex machina* does not come to secure Zingis' love life (for Zingis had already done so with his sword), but he returns to him the sister who was believed to be dead. He appears

as an old man and tells Zingis that Axione is actually his (Zingis')
sister. She is alive and is about to marry one of his friends.
Finally free from the torment of believing his sister was dead, and
after the triple wedding—Zingis to Taxila, Philing to Axione and
Omir to Thamirise—Zingis surely finds complete happiness.

The *deus ex machina* does not show himself in *Le Grand
Scanderberg*, for he is not needed. Scanderberg, who proves
himself to be even mightier than Zingis, earns his happiness by
way of the sword. Scanderberg attacks the king, Amurat, who is
holding Arianisse captive, just in time to save Arianisse's father's
life. However, in the meantime, Musulman, one of Scanderberg's
rivals, has kidnapped Arianisse. Scanderberg goes off to find him;
Musulman too is killed.

It is clear that cause and effect and the flashback play an
important role in the plot of the novels of Anne de la Roche-
Guilhen. In each of the three novels, *Almanzaïde, Le Grand
Scanderberg*, and *Zingis*, there is a chain reaction that takes place
commencing with the very first incident. A good illustration is the
note that Cleonis writes to Almanzor asking him to meet her
secretly so that they may talk. Roxane sees the note and concludes
that Almanzor and Cleonis are having an affair. She tells the king
about her suspicions, while showing him the letter. The king
finally believes Roxane's suspicions and gives the order to kill
both Almanzor and Cleonis. Toxare, a slave, is killed instead of
Almanzor. Thus, this single note causes many effects, even a
man's death.

The flashback plays a role equal to, if not greater than, that of
cause and effect in the plot of la Roche-Guilhen's novels. In
Zingis, which is a one hundred sixty page novel, there are three
flashbacks, in story form, that cover a total of one hundred
nineteen pages. The flashbacks in *Almanzaïde* and *Le Grand
Scanderberg* are equally lengthy. The story of Almanzor and
Almanzaïde is forty-three pages long; the story of the birth of
Almanzor and Almanzaïde is twenty-three pages long; the story of
Scanderberg is seventy-five pages long; the story of Thopia is
twenty-six pages long.

Anne de la Roche-Guilhen

The *deus ex machina* is that all powerful being who swoops down and saves the hero's life and solves all of his problems. He makes an appearance, as a stranger, in two of the above novels. While bringing good but unexpected news, this stranger solves the problem that is the only remaining hindrance to the happiness of the couple in question, and everyone lives happily every after.

La Roche-Guilhen's Originality

Clearly, the plots of Anne de la Roche-Guilhen are not as complex as those of many of her contemporaries. Although she used some of the same novelistic conventions employed by other seventeenth-century novelists, she did not adhere to their tendency to utilize these devices abusively. In Madame de Villedieu's *Alcidamie* (1661) for example, one encounters " . . . les nauf-frages, les pirates, les iles désertes, les substitutions d'enfants, de la tradition romanesque, les batailles, les sièges, [et] les combats singuliers dont La Calprenède avait fait un si grand abus" (Adam 4:160). Of these inventions, la Roche-Guilhen used only the military battles and the substitution of infants.

Shipwrecks are an element of plot that appears quite frequently in the works of many seventeenth-century novelists, but the three novels of Anne de la Roche-Guilhen that are used in this study are devoid of this device. Mlle de Scudéry, for instance, makes use of novelistic conventions such as storms, shipwrecks, and pirates. Even in Madame de La Fayette's *Zaïde* there are " . . . naviga-tions, des naufrages, des existence vouées à la guerre et à l'amour, des joutes, des tournois . . ." (Adam 4:181). For the most part, these shipwrecks, among some of the other devices, are not found in the novels of Anne de la Roche-Guilhen because in her works, the action basically centers around the home of the hero and heroine. Furthermore, when the hero does venture away from home, usually to do battle, he goes no further than a neighboring country. Moreover, la Roche-Guilhen tends to keep the feet of her characters on land. When her characters do encounter great bodies of water, however, they are either fishing or taking a pleasant boat ride on a peaceful lake or river. Although Mlle de la Roche-Guilhen's characters do not have to contend with the raging sea, they do, on several occasions, find themselves in trouble on water. Frequently, the heroine's boat overturns; she nearly drowns, and the hero comes to her rescue.

Since la Roche-Guilhen did not write interminable *romans*, as did La Calprenède and Mlle de Scudéry, she was not forced to make excessive use of conventions such as kidnappings and shipwrecks in order to fill volumes. La Roche-Guilhen's novels are composed of rather simple plots—the prince is finally free to love the princess because of his persistence. Although there are several subplots in each of la Roche-Guilhen's works, they are somehow interrelated with the main plot. The narration found in the works of those authors who chose to employ novelistic conventions excessively is quite often confusing to the reader. For example, in Gomberville's novels, " . . . la narration devient proprement inextricable. Les innombrables déplacements sur terre et sur mer achèvent de désorienter le lecteur" (Lever 112).

Like her contemporaries, Anne de la Roche-Guilhen chose historical figures, in most cases, as her main characters, but she made no effort to portray them in their true historical surroundings. Once she has chosen a recognizable historical name for her character and has briefly explained who this particular character is according to history, she makes no further mention of historical fact. Instead, she creates an imaginary world, not without the problems one confronts in everyday life, where love reigns supreme. Her hero is mainly seen reacting to the effects of being in love while the kings, though they may also fight battles and give orders to have innocent people executed, act as a counter force, interfering with the hero's efforts to find happiness.

In spite of the many similarities in the novels produced during the seventeenth century, each novelist tends to have a particular trait that distinguishes him from all others. La Calprenède, having served in the French armed forces, revealed " . . . un réel souci d'exactitude dans tout ce qui touche à l'art de la guerre" (Lever 121). The novels of Mlle de Scudéry, who " . . . analyze, avec beaucoup de charme et de finesse, les melancolies douces, les rêveries tristes et touchantes . . ." (Adam 2:139), expose the charm of conversations, portraits of contemporary celebrities in historical settings and heroes whose names are known to all. Madame de La Fayette's " . . . individuality is most sharply emphasized . . . in the moral purpose which reveals itself in all her novels . . ." (Green 46-47). Moreover, it is by way of her pen that the psychological novel is born. The novels of Mme de Villedieu " . . . affect, of the most part, the form of mémoires. They reflect the daily life of the polite society of their day, but their chief concern is amorous adventure" (Green 57). Anne de la Roche-Guilhen's unique treatment of love distinguishes her novels from those of other seventeenth-century writers. She portrays love as a monstrous force that has complete control over the lives of its victims.

Love is also the principal theme in Mlle de Scudéry's novels, but Scudéry emphasizes the different stages of love and the many emotional dangers encountered when one is in love. She even draws the plans for the famous "Carte de Tendre" which shows the different means of finding perfect happiness. Nevertheless, Scudéry makes it quite clear that few couples find this perfect happiness and adds that there are even other dangers after finding it. Thus, Scudéry is more concerned with rules that one must follow to obtain some form of happiness than with the actual effect love has on those who are enamored.

On the contrary, Anne de la Roche-Guilhen treats only the effect love has on its victims. She reveals the actions and reactions of her characters. Characterisitically, love has a more passionate portrayal in the works of la Roche-Guilhen than in those of Mlle de Scudéry. In la Roche-Guilhen's novels, the reader witnesses the sadness, the jealousy, the self-sacrificing attitude, the will to kill and the passionate emotion that love brings upon its victims. It is actually love that causes her characters to act. This special treatment of love-passion in her characters distinguishes her among her contemporaries, for they too made use of devices of plot such as cause and effect, and the flashback. The effect love has on la Roche-Guilhen's characters will be examined more closely in the chapter that follows.

Chapter Three

Characterization: The Hero, Heroine, King and Queen in the Works of Anne de la Roche-Guilhen

A writer may choose one of two ways to present his characters: he may describe them in a "set piece" or "unroll" them (Macauley and Lanning 61). When characters are displayed as a "set piece", the narrator usually discloses their physical features as well as their character-traits within a few paragraphs. Thus, if an author introduces his personage in a "set piece", the reader is given a preconceived description of the particular character's appearance along with that of the distinguishing features of his personality. Consequently, having completed the shaping of his persona, the writer is forced to create a story that conforms with his "set piece". In contrast, if a writer chooses to "unroll" his characters, quite often nothing or very little is said about their appearance or disposition at the outset of the novel. It is while reading the novel (or other literary form) that one grasps a full understanding of the "unrolled" character. Hence, as in real life, character is judged by what the personage says, what he does, what others say about him and by what others do because of him.

In the novels of Anne de la Roche-Guilhen, the characters are "unrolled". Occasionally, it may be mentioned that the prince is gallant or that the princess is beautiful, but nothing else is said at the outset about any of their distinguishing physical features or personal qualities.

The Hero

In Anne de la Roche-Guilhen's novels, the hero is always a highly respected prince who appears to be a "superman"—able to conquer any problem. He is oftentimes a warrior who is invariably victorious in battle, and a lover who consistantly gets the princess that he loves. The hero in *Le Grand Scanderberg* is a prince by birth, but because his father is afraid of Amurat's military strength, he gives Scanderberg and his three brothers to king Amurat as a peace offering. Scanderberg is very young when he arrives in Amurat's court. His three brothers are immediately enslaved, but Scanderberg finds favor with the king and is treated as the king's own son.

Like Scanderberg, the hero in *Zingis* is also a prince by birth. However, during his youth he decides to go away to do battle in order to earn a name for himself. Once he has accomplished his goal, Zingis goes to Undkan's palace to see his father. Undkan invites him to stay, and Zingis accepts. While serving in Undkan's army, Zingis proves himself worthy of the great name he has gained by the sword.

Almanzor the hero of *Almanzaïde*, like Scanderberg, finds himself in slavery. Actually, he is the king's son, but the truth is not discovered until the end of the novel. The king, Abdala, has two wives, one of whom is extremely jealous. So, it is decided that the child's death would be feigned at birth so that he may be sent from the castle to be reared elsewhere. During his youth, he is returned to the castle as a slave. Nevertheless, like la Roche-Guilhen's other heroes, he is never treated as a slave.

Thus, in each case, treated like royalty even though he is supposedly a slave, the hero possesses qualities of a true prince. A prisoner in a subservient position, but fighting with valor and using his wit, he is able to overcome his slavery and elevate himself to the royal status that is rightfully his. Moreover, two of these heroes are separated from their parents during their youth: when he was only eight years old, Scanderberg is given to king Amurat; during his infancy, Almanzor is taken from his father's castle.

In spite of the fact that the heroes are often denied the opportunity to enjoy close family ties during their youth, and although they must serve a king in a foreign land, they all excel rapidly. As Scanderberg tells his friend Thopia, by the time he is nineteen years old, he has already been named commander of five thousand soldiers: ". . . à dix-neuf ans Amurat me fit Sangiac, c'est à dire Conducteur, me donna cinq mille chevaux à commander. Fort peu de temps aprés, je fus nommé Bassa, dignité qui me soumettoit des Sangiacs" (la Roche-Guilhen 17). When Zingis is only three years old, his mother's health begins to fail, and she dies soon thereafter. Thus, Zingis is reared by brigands.

Because of their many heroic deeds, the heroes are all held in high esteem by their captors. Upon their arrival in their new homeland, they receive special treatment and privileges from the kings. It appears that these great princes have some hypnotic power that controls the king's ability to love or hate, for in each case, the hero is loved by his captor. Quite often, the king gives the hero the best of everything—most of all, the best possible education. Scanderberg's education is placed in the hands of king Amurat's very capable slave, Aradin. While speaking to his friend Thopia, Scanderberg gives the reader some idea of the quality of his education: "Je ne vous dirai point ce que je fis depuis huit ans jusqu'à seize; j'apris les exercises du corps, & les choses utiles à l'esprit; Aradin n'oublia rien pour me faire aimer la gloire & la vertu" (16).

Thus, Scanderberg finds himself in the camp of his people's enemy being taught how to fight, how to love and seek those qualities befitting a great man. He takes full advantage of this opportunity, and after several important military victories, king Amurat calls Scanderberg "son bras droit, son coeur, son oeil, & le deffenseur de ses Etats" (17).

Almanzor also receives a very good education from his captor.

He, like la Roche-Guilhen's other heroes, is taught in such a manner that he may become an *honnête homme*: ". . . il [Almanzor] tenoit une education avantageuse, & la connoissance de toutes les Sciences qui peuvent former l'esprit d'un honneste homme" (la Roche-Guilhen 8). King Abdala loves Almanzor and he often overlooks others in order to honor Almanzor: "Il [king Abdala] l'aima tendrement, & fit toûjours [sic] une obligeante distinction de luy avec les autres. Il voulut mesme qu'il portast le nom d'Almanzor, celebre [sic] dans le royaume de Maroc, pour avoir esté donné à plusieurs de leurs Roys" (5-6).

Contrary to the personal relationship between Scanderberg and Almanzor and their respective captors, Zingis' relationship with king Undkan is quite distant. Nevertheless, Undkan does love him, but only out of gratitude and respect. Moreover, Zingis is not educated by Undkan, but he is first taught at home by his father, and then goes off to get experience on the battle field in foreign lands. Therefore, when Zingis arrives in Undkan's camp, he is already a great warrior. Undkan does not have the opportunity to watch Zingis grow from a child to a man, and they are both adults when they meet for the first time. Nevertheless, once in Undkan's camp, Zingis quickly gains his love, respect and friendship. Zingis earns his glory by leading the king's army to victory and saving Undkan's life: ". . . il [Zingis] sauva la vie à Undkan, qui se trouva engagé malgré lui parmi les Ennemis, & aprés plusieurs batailles, il fit les trois Rois prisonniers en differentes occasions, ce qui termina la guerre de ce côté" (la Roche-Guilhen 49).

Anne de la Roche-Guilhen's hero is always in love with some beautiful princess. Usually the reader is given the opportunity to witness the hero's first encounter with the young maiden who becomes the object of his love. He is most often caught off guard; once he meets this innocent princess, all hope to escape is lost. He is immediately captivated by her beauty. She does not, however, respond favorably to his advances at first. Before admitting that she loves the prince, she seems to go through some strange ritual, for she tells the him that she can not return his love for various reasons and that he should turn his attention to some other princess who is truly worthy of him. Nevertheless, the prince persists and eventually succeeds.

Scanderberg, unlike Zingis or Almanzor, falls in love with Arianisse even before he sees her. He hears her voice one day and he is immediately mesmerized. While reminiscing, Scanderberg says: ". . . je peux dire que je fus amoureux sans avoir vû ce que j'aimais" (29). Throughout this novel, Scanderberg is seen as a strong hero who seems to be able to win any battle. However, when he encounters love, his extremely powerful opponent, he is utterly helpless. The narrator explains that

> . . . l'Amour fit ce que tous ses ennemis n'avoient pú [sic] faire. Il perça de plusieurs traits le coeur de l'invulnérable Scanderberg; & Arianisse, toute esclave qu'elle étoit, chargea de fers le Vainqueur du plus puissant Empereur du Monde. (4)

Zingis succumbs to the mighty flames of love as quickly as Scanderberg. Upon his arrival, Zingis sees Taxila, the princess who captures his heart, for the first time in the garden of the palace. He is in the midst of a duel with Timur who is trying to chase Zingis out of the garden which is forbidden to men. Suddenly, Zingis notices Taxila. He freezes in his tracks—sword in hand. Timur's life is saved only because Zingis is captivated by the beauty of Taxila; otherwise, Zingis would have certainly killed him. Later, Zingis openly expresses his love for Taxila before the crowd that assembles to watch his execution:

> O Taxila! dit-il assez haut, je vous donne ma vie d'aussi bon coeur que j'aurois fait l'empire de l'Univers, s'il avoit été en mon pouvoir. Recevez-là [sic] comme une preuve certaine de mon amour fidelle, & souvenez-vous de Zingis. (116)

Almanzor, the third hero, falls in love with Almanzaïde during their youth. Even though he is quite young when he first meets her, he develops a desire to be with her at all times and takes advantages of every opportunity to do so. Almanzor wants to inform Almanzaïde of his feelings for her, but he refuses to do so at first because he is afraid she will not readily accept him as a lover. Nevertheless, he finally decides to confess his true feelings to her. Once he has revealed his long-kept secret, our hero is determined to have Almanzaïde as his own. He proclaims that he would rather die than live without her: "Que vous estes obstiné, reprit Almanzaïde, & que j'auray de peine à vous vaincre? Ne l'esperez iamais, poursuivis-je, puis qu'il seroit égal pour moi de mourir ou de cesser de vous aimer" (52).

Being in love has many effects on Mademoiselle de la Roche-Guilhen's heroes. The most obvious of these effects is sadness. Each of her heroes is sad throughout most of the novel. Once he overcomes his mistress's resistance, the hero always finds that there is another obstacle. In many cases, when he is confronted with this effectual snag, he simply gives up all hope and plunges into a deep melancholic state.

The narrator in *Le Grand Scanderberg* gives a very clear description of the role love plays in that particular novel. It is a villain who while sneaking up on its unsuspecting victims, bringing them pain and sorrow, quickly overpowers its prey and gains complete control over him. The narrator describes it thus:

> Scanderberg depuis son retour, y [à Croye] passoit une vie que l'on auroit pú dire heureuse, si l'amour n'avoit pas mêlé ses plus noirs chagrins, à l'avantage de régner dans les coeurs de tous ses sujets, comme sur des Royaumes assez vastes. (6)

Since Scanderberg falls in love with Arianisse before he meets her face to face, he is tormented for an extended period of time. Actually, he falls in love with her voice, and he is immediately troubled by the fact that he has not seen her. He becomes obsessed with the idea of meeting the person who owns this beautiful voice. He finally meets her accidently and she is more beautiful than he has ever imagined. Consequently, he loves Arianisse even more.

Scanderberg, like the other heroes, has a rival. In fact, he eventually discovers that he has three rivals: the Emperor Amurat, the prince Mahomet and Musulman. Finally, Scanderberg's rivals make their feelings known to Arianisse who does not readily respond to either of them. Later, she reveals that she prefers Scanderberg, but she realizes that she will have to accept Amurat as a suitor since he far outranks the others. When Amurat discovers that he has rivals and that Arianisse prefers Scanderberg, he has Scanderberg thrown in prison while he simply reprimands Mahomet and Musulman—hence, Amurat finds Scanderberg to be a greater threat than his other rivals. Neverthesless, Scanderberg has become such a great hero in the eyes of the people that Amurat is forced to set him free.

Zingis meets Taxila when he wanders into a garden forbidden to men. It is love at first sight. Zingis, a strong valiant soldier, is powerless when confronted with the bitter-sweet joy love brings. Moreover, he finds that Taxila is not free to return his love, for she has been promised to Timur, the son of the king's second wife. Once he learns that Zingis is in love with Taxila, Timur sets out to rid himself of this worthy rival. He goes to his mother who promises to solve the problem. She forces the king to finalize the plans for Timur's marriage; Zingis attacks and nearly kills Timur. Consequently, Zingis is forced to flee the country, leaving his beloved Taxila behind.

Likewise, Almanzor finds himself in love with a beautiful princess who is not free to love him. From the very beginning of the novel, the reader is made aware of the fact that Almanzor is in an extremely sad state of mind: ". . . il tomba dans une mélancholie qui parut à tous ses amis mais particulierement au premier des Eunuques d'Abdala" (8). Aristan notices Almanzor's sadness, and begs him to explain his unusual disposition. After hesitating for quite some time, Almanzor finally shares his secret with Aristan. Almanzor explains that:

> . . . le Prince Abdemar, fils du Roy, & de la fiere Roxane,
> est son [Almanzaïde's] amant aussi bien qu'Almanzor; C'est
> ce Rival qui me rend infortuné; c'est luy qui envieux des
> avantages que l'amour me donne sur le coeur d'Alman-
> zaïde, par une cruelle jalousie, trouble deux personnes que
> le ciel a fait naistre pour s'aimer. (19-20)

Thus, we find that Almanzor is depressed because he is in love;
we also discover that the main cause of his sadness is the fact that
he has a rival. Abdemar, the king's son and Almanzor's rival,
learns that Almanzor is in love with Almanzaïde and immediately
makes plans to keep Almanzor away from her. Almanzor is so
determinded, however, that Abdemar does not succeed.

After hearing that Almanzor is in love with Almanzaïde,
Aristan is very distraught. He tries to convince Almanzor that
Almanzaïde is not worthy of him. He explains that she is only a
slave, and that although he is also a slave, Almanzor has earned
the right to choose any woman he pleases. This does not alter
Almanzor's desire to have Almanzaïde as his own; so finally,
Aristan decides that he must tell Almanzor the truth. The truth,
however, is only another burden that Almanzor must endure.
Almanzor and Almanzaïde are brother and sister. When Almanzor
hears this news, he is totally devastated. He even remains in his
room for three days. He is unable to accept the truth and insists
that he must have Almanzaïde in spite of the fact that she is his
sister. He confesses his unceasing love for her only to find that
she is willing to accept this awful truth (that they are sister and
brother) and forget about him. Therefore, he gets angry and
accuses Almanzaïde of never really loving him. He is vexed by
the ease with which Almanzaïde overcomes her feelings for him
while he is unable to forget her. Fortunately, Almanzor finally
learns that he is not Almanzaïde's brother after all. Otherwise, it
appears that Almanzor would inevitably become insane.

In Anne de la Roche-Guilhen's novels, the heroine plays a very
important role in the life of the hero. Once the hero has fallen in
love with her, she becomes a life sustaining force. Everything he

does thereafter is designed to please her. He goes off to battle to prove himself worthy of her; he leaves the country at her request; he risks his life to see her or he spares her father's life for her sake; and when given an opportunity, the hero is always willing to risk his own life to save that of his mistress.

Scanderberg saves Arianisse's life twice. Once, while on the shore of a river, he notices a woman who is drowning. Without hesitating, he jumps in to save her. When he takes the woman from the water, he realizes that it is Arianisse. On this particular occasion, Scanderberg does not recognize the woman in the water, but he is still willing to risk his life to save her—unselfish gallantry .

Scanderberg risks his life a second time to save Arianisse when the building in which Arianisse lives is engulfed in flames. On this occasion, realizing that it is Arianisse's life that he must save and seeing that she, as well as others, is about to be consumed by the fire, Scanderberg forgets the harm he may bring upon himself by attempting to rescue Arianisse, and goes into the burning building walking on hot coals: ". . . je marchai sur des morceaux de cendres brûlantes jusques à une galerie . . . je courus à Arianisse . . ." (83). The king and many soldiers were at the scene before Scanderberg's arrival, but none of them were brave enough to try to save anyone.

Zingis also risks his life to save Taxila. As he sees the boat in which Taxila is riding overturn, Zingis immediately, without considering the danger, plunges into the water and saves Taxila's life:

> . . . mais le courageus Zingis animé par d'autres sentiments se precipita dans le fleuve, & coupant adroitement le cours de l'eau, il reçut la princesse dans ses bras au moment qu'elle revint dessus, & qu'elle alloit peutêtre retomber pour toûjours au fonds du fleuve. Son action fut si prompte, que nul autre ne le put devancer. (30)

Anne de la Roche-Guilhen's hero is nearly always an invincible warrior. No task is impossible for him. He leads the army to victory, killing men and sparing lives at will. Scanderberg is unquestionably this type of hero. He fights to win. On one occasion, he kills almost two thousand men with his own hands without receiving a single wound: ". . . l'invincible Scanderberg . . . Ce redoutable Capitaine, qui ne combattoit jamais que pour remporter la victoire, tua prés [sic] de deux mille Turcs de sa main, sans recevoir jamais aucune blessure . . ." (4). Scanderberg is a gallant warrior who wins many battles and conquers many provinces while earning a great name for himself. It is even predicted that he would be a great conquerer; his mother had a dream which was interpreted to mean that he would conquer the Turkish people. It is ironic that he enters Turkey as a youth and is taught how to fight only to grow up to use that knowledge against the country that trained him.

Zingis is also portrayed as a very gallant warrior who because of his deeds as a soldier is referred to as a supernatural being: ". . . on peut dire qu'il [Zingis] paroissoit quelque chose de plus qu'humain" (19). He goes off to war alongside Undkan and leads the army to victory over three kings. During this particular battle, he also saves Undkan's life. When he learns that another group of Undkan's soldiers was being pursued by one of their enemies, he goes to its rescue, and leads the soldiers to victory.

To the contrary, Almanzor does not so much as lift a sword in *Almanzaïde*. He is never seen on the battlefield and he never plans to go. All of his time is spent trying to secure a place for himself in Almanzaïde's heart. If he is to be classified as an invincible warrior, it must be based on his many achievements on the battlefield of love. Almanzaïde is a very capable opponent. She is able to resist Almanzor's many advances with ease. Nevertheless, he finally conquers her: "Almanzaïde vaincuë ne combatit plus tant ce que ie voulus luy dire & ie goûtay la ioye que peut inspirer la persuasion d'estre aimé" (53).

Bravery is another characteristic that is highly visible in our author's hero. He is usually willing to sacrifice himself in order to help others. He is never afraid to fight a battle regardless of the odds against him, and he will gladly fight a duel with any man who has the nerve to challenge him. Scanderberg shows his bravery on the battlefield and by saving his beloved's life. Zingis exemplifies his bravery very much in the same way. He saves the king's life, captures three kings and saves his beloved's life. Since Almanzor does not go onto the battlefield and is not given the opportunity to save Almanzaïde's life, he does not display any bravery at all. Nevertheless, he is not portrayed as a coward.

The reader does not have to search for adjectives to describe the personal character-traits of Anne de la Roche-Guilhen's hero, for the narrators in each novel provide an ample supply, and the hero's actions suggest many others. The hero is generally depicted as the perfect demigod who has no real flaws. In the preface of *Le Grand Scanderberg*, Anne de la Roche-Guilhen describes Scanderberg, the hero, as a man who has no faults: ". . . l'amour ne lui fait rien dire, ni rien faire qui soit indigne de lui". She explains that love is a powerful force that has brought many great men and even some gods to their destruction. Scanderberg, however, as Mademoiselle de la Roche-Guilhen explains, is able to maintain his levelheadness even though he is subjected to the great power of love. The narrator tells us that Scanderberg is also one of the most generous men who ever lived: "La valeur & la générosité n'ont jamais paru avec tant d'éclat, qu'en la personne de l'invincible Scanderberg . . . des moeurs sans deffauts; & sa vertu peut servir d'exemple à tous les souvenirs du monde" (5). One may also conclude that Scanderberg is a little selfish, for he climbs the social ladder while his brothers remain slaves; he does nothing to free them from slavery. He admits, however, that their slavery causes him grief from time to time, and that since he does not see them suffer, he is able to ignore their enslavement and pursue his goals: "L'Esclavage de mes freres me donnoit des momens de chagrin; mais outre que je ne les voyois pas souffrir, dans le dessein que j'avois de me faire un avenir Illustre, rien n'étoit capable de m'arrêter" (17-18). Although Scanderberg is portrayed as an invincible soldier or superman, he is unable to hide his emotions when he says goodbye to Arianisse: ". . . pour

moi, j'embrassai les genoux d'Arianisse; j'y repandis des larmes"
(86). Thus, we find that Scanderberg, is only human after all.

In spite of the fact that he too is a great hero, Zingis is
portrayed as a respectful, merciful and kindhearted man. Once he
has fallen in love with Taxila, Zingis shows the greatest possible
respect throughout all of his dealings with her:

> Zingis avoit trop de respect pour ne s'imposer pas une
> parfaite discretion: quoi qu'il fut Prince, et en état de
> prétendre à toutes choses, il ne précipita point une déclara-
> tion de son amour, qui pouvoit irriter Taxila, & voulut
> attendre que ses services la preparassent à l'écouter favora-
> blement. (27)

Zingis does not tell Taxila of his feelings for her until he is
convinced that she is mentally prepared to hear it. He chooses to
suffer, keeping his love a secret, rather than burden Taxila.

Zingis' mercifulness is shown on two occasions. When he
leads Undkan's soldiers to victory and captures three kings,
Undkan gives him the right to decide the fate of his captives.
Zingis not only spares their lives, but he also sets them free
requiring only that they pay an annual tribute. On another occasion, Zingis saves Undkans's life by stopping one of his soldiers
from killing Undkan while fighting to free Zingis from the
execution that has been arranged by Undkan himself. Zingis
reveals his kindheartedness when he is encouraged by his soldiers
to enter Undkan's palace with military force. He refuses to do so
because he does not want to embarrass Unkan, even though
Undkan had put him in prison and planned to execute him.

One of Almanzor's strongest character-traits is his obstinancy.
From the beginning of their acquaintance, Almanzor decides that
he must have Almanzaïde as his own. In spite of the many
obstacles that confront him, he never gives up. Even when he is
told that she is his sister, although devastated at first, he goes to
her and tells her that he still loves her. While hoping that Almanzaïde feels the same way, it appears that Almanzor is willing to

ignore the fact that they are brother and sister. Moreover, the reader is informed by Almanzaïde herself that Almanzor is obstinate: "Que vous estes obstiné, reprit Almanzaïde . . ." (52).

Another of Almanzor's personal character-traits is craftiness. Abdemar, his rival, does everything within his power to ban Almanzor from Almanzaïde's presence. Nevertheless, Almanzor finds a way to see and speak with her. The reader is given an opportunity to hear Almanzor himself boast about his dexterity: ". . . mais malgré luy ie trouvay toujours des momens favorable de voir, & d'entretenir Almanzaïde" (56).

The Heroine

The heroine in the works of Anne de la Roche-Guilhen is portrayed as a delicate, caring, and virtuous young maiden. Although she may not be aware of it at first, she is always a princess. Since the heroine is of royal blood, one may assume that she is very happy. On the contrary, each of la Roche-Guilhen's heroines is a captive in one sense or another. Arianisse, the heroine in *Le Grand Scanderberg*, is Amurat's captive. Amurat is in love with her and wants to marry her, but Arianisse wants no part of him. Therefore, she is forced to live in a virtual hell, where she is tortured by her repugnant captor who tries constantly to persuade her to return his love. Taxila, the heroine in *Zingis*, is the daughter of Undkan, who has remarried and has promised his new wife that he will give Taxila to her son, Timur, in marriage. Taxila does not love Timur at all; in fact, she grows to hate him. Throughout the novel, Taxila is tormented by the thought of having to marry him. The heroine in *Almanzaïde* is given to Roxane, one of king Abdala's wives, as a slave. Roxane's son, Abdemar, is in love with Almanzaïde, the heroine, but of course she does not love him. Thus, Roxane and Abdemar join forces in an effort to find a way to get rid of Almanzor, the young prince with whom Almanzaïde is in love. Consequently, Almanzaïde, afraid some harm may come to Almanzor because of her refusal to love Abdemar, is forced to lead a life filled with pain and suffering.

Anne de la Roche-Guilhen's heroine is always in love with some gallant prince—her knight in shining armor. The heroine's beauty is rarely described. In *Zingis*, the reader finds a description of Taxila: "La Princesse de Tartarie étoit née avec des qualitez admirables. On n'a jamais vu de si beau qu'elle. Les charmes de son esprit égaloient ceux de sa beauté" (4). The heroine is consistently the most beautiful young princess in the land. It seems that no one can deny her this superior status, for all men are captivated by her beauty even though only a few dare inform her of their affection. As mentioned in the description above, the heroine's beauty is much more than physical attractiveness.

The heroine in the works of la Roche-Guilhen is quite sensitive and usually cries at some point during the unfolding of the plot. She is most often very delicate and virtuous. In some cases, however, the heroine may appear very strong and levelheaded. In the end, the reader learns, however, that this is only a façade. In *Le Grand Scanderberg*, Arianisse's sensitivity is revealed when Scanderberg tells her that he must leave in order to avenge his family's honor. When he tells her about the condition of his family—his father is dead; his brothers have been enslaved; his mother has been robbed of all her possessions and dignity, and is living somewhere in Albania with her daughters—Arianisse begins to cry, and reluctantly tells Scanderberg to go avenge his family's name: "Mon discours toucha Arianisse, par des endroits sensibles; & ses larmes me le firent connoître. Allez, Seigneur, me dit-elle tristement, allez en Albanie; vangez votre Sang . . ." (86).

When Taxila discovers that Zingis has been captured by her father, Undkan, she is overcome with grief and begins to cry. She is in love with Zingis, who has been banished from her country because it was disclosed that he and Taxila love each other. Taxila realizes that Zingis' capture will probably lead to his death, and the thought of losing him forever proves to be too much to bear: "L'affligée Taxila accompagnoit ces paroles d'un torrent de larmes" (7). We observe Almanzaïde's sensitivity when Roxane criticizes her for being in love with Almanzor: "Almanzaïde avoit le coeur trop sensible pour souffrir patiemment le discours de Roxane, elle connoissoit son innocence, & avoit toujours vescu avec Almanzor d'une maniere à meriter plûtost des loüanges que des reproches . . ." (129).

The personal character-traits of two of la Roche-Guilhen's heroines are described in detail by the various narrators in the novels. However, no indepth description of Arianisse is given. The reader can only speculate in regard to her character-traits. The fact that Scanderberg, along with three other men, is in love with Arianisse in addition to Scanderberg's repeated references to her beauty indicate that she is indeed very enchanting. Otherwise, the reader only learns that she is levelheaded and lovable, and is born into a royal family. Arianisse uses her wit when she receives a letter from Scanderberg. She refuses to accept the letter at first because she is afraid the king sent it to test her loyalty. Moreover, when she finally reads the letter, she sends a message to Scanderberg telling him to forget about her.

In *Zingis*, one learns that Taxila is a virtuous, charming, forgiving young woman who is greatly admired. She is also born into a royal family and has the qualities of a goddess: "Elle avoit l'ame [sic] grande, une vertu parfaite, & l'on peut dire que le Ciel ne lui avoit rien épargné" (4). Taxila is also very compassionate. She does not delight in the death of Timur even though she hated him, and his death means that she will not have to marry him after all: ". . . elle n'aimoit pas le sang, la mort de Timur ne lui fit pas de plaisir, quelque avantage qu'elle pût recevoir" (121).

Almanzaïde is portrayed as a virtuous, generous, delicate young princess who has high self-esteem. When Roxane tries to convince Almanzaïde that Almanzor is not worthy of her, Almanzaïde protests with vigor:

Ie n'ay point fait de choix indigne, madame, & malgré l'obscurité de ma naissance, me connoissant une ame assez élevée; j'ay laissé au Ciel le soin de ma destinée. I'espere qu'il la protegera, & qu'il permettra que ie me iustifie. (132-133)

Almanzaïde is convinced that she is not a slave even though she is serving in that capacity. On another occasion, she asserts that she does not feel that she was born a slave. She explains that she does not like being a servant at all:

> Pour moy, ajoûta-t-elle avec le malheur d'une naissance inconnuë, i'ay celuy d'estre captive; mais Almanzor ie sens, & ie connois mon coeur, & tout ce qu'il m'inspire est si élevé, que malgré l'estat où ie me vois une fierté naturelle qui me fait envisager tout, ce qui tient de la bassesse avec horreur, me persuade que ie ne suis point inferieure à Roxane. (33-34)

Almanzaïde's delicateness is exposed when she hears from Roxane that Almanzor and Cleonis are lovers—which is not true—and that the king has given the order to have them both killed. Deeply in love with Almanzor, Almanzaïde is unable to readily accept the idea that Almanzor is in love with another, nor is she able to accept the thought of his being put to death: ". . . elle [Almanzaïde] tomba sur un lict de repos auprés [sic] duquel elle estoit, sans force, & sans couleur" (164). At the end of the novel, we discover that Almanzaïde is also very generous. When it is revealed that she is a princess about to be crowned as queen of her native country, Almanzaïde tells Almanzor that it would all be meaningless to her unless she is able to share it with him. He accepts. When she receives the royal crown, she places it on his head, giving him all the authority that goes with it. Almanzor himself gives the most complete description of Almanzaïde:

> . . . il n'y a point au monde de vertu plus solide que la sienne, elle a une generosité sans exemple, des sentimens si nobles, un discernement si delicat, & un tour d'esprit si peu ordinaire, que l'on peut dire hardiment que ses plus grandes beautez sont inconnuës à ceux qui n'ont pas avec elle ces conversations familieres dans lesquelles on parle avec liberté. (22-23)

The King

All of the kings in *Le Grand Scanderberg*, *Zingis*, and *Alman-zaïde* are portrayed as weak and cowardly men. In many instances, they appear to be unable to make important decisions. They are controlled by their wives who tend to totally dominate them. However, Amurat, the king in *Le Grand Scanderberg*, is an exeption to this general trend, for he does not have a wife—at least, there is no mention of one in the novel. Consequently, Amurat is not portrayed as a henpecked husband, but his coward-ice is quite evident. When Scanderberg and his army arrive in Amurat's camp, they conquer Amurat's soldiers without difficulty. When Amurat realizes that his army is losing the battle, he decides to flee to safety: "Amurat qui se vit sans espoir de vaincre, courut à la Tente d'Arianisse avec de funestes résolutions . . ." (112).

When Undkan sees that his wife is happy to learn that Zingis will be executed, he begins to rejoice with her: "Le foible Undkan se laissoit entraîner aux mêmes movemens . . ." (114). He appears to be afraid to show any emotions that oppose those of his wife. Furthermore, Undkan is terrified when he sees that Zingis' army is about to destroy all of his soldiers during the battle to set Zingis free: "Undkan fut ému de plusieurs passions à la fois, & le timide Roi de Tenduc pâlit de crainte, ne doutant pas qu'il ne fut obligé de s'exposer à la valeur de Zingis, qui lui étoit si connuë" (118). Instead of fighting with his soldiers until death, Undkan runs into his palace only to be followed by the other kings who were visiting him: "Undkan . . . peut-être, le moins lâche de ces Rois, sortit; les autres le suiverent . . ." (119).

Like Undkan, Abdala, the king in *Almanzaïde*, is greatly influenced by his evil wife, Roxane, who seems to have some mystical power over him, for he always tries to give her what she wants, even if he does not agree with it. For example, when Roxane gives Abdala the note that Cleonis, Abdala's other wife, wrote to Almanzor, she persuades him to believe that Cleonis and Almanzor are having an affair. Abdala finally accepts Roxane's insinuation as the truth, and without questioning Cleonis or

Almanzor, he gives the order to have them both killed.

Although Abdala is portrayed as a man dominated by his wife, he does not appear to be a coward. All of Roxane's evil acts are committed without his knowledge, and considering his reaction when he finds out what Roxane has done (attempted to take Cleonis' life, and lied about Cleonis and Almanzor being lovers, nearly causing their death), it becomes apparent that Abdala would have stopped her had he been aware of her diabolical scheme. Perhaps Abdala is not perceived as a coward because he does not fight any battles. The reader is most often made aware of the cowardliness of the other kings, Amurat and Undkan, when they are confronted with life-threatening situations.

These kings all have a tendency to be very cruel, especially when angry. Amurat's cruelty is displayed in Arianisse's room once he finds out that he has rivals; after terrorizing the guards, Amurat places them at the door of Arianisse's room and instructs them not to allow anyone to enter:

> Amurat manaça les Eunuques & jetta la terreur par tout: Il fit passer les plus vieux de son serrail à la garde des femmes, & l'on en mit un si grand nombre auprés [sic] de l'apartement d'Arianisse, que l'entrée en devint inaccessible. (74)

On another occasion, Amurat is angered by Arianisse's refusal to love him. Thus, he threatens to kill her father in a public execution if she continues to reject him. Amurat prepares to carry out his threat, and forces Arianisse to watch. Undoubtedly, he hopes that she will be persuaded to change her mind, but on the contrary, Arianisse faints, and shortly thereafter Scanderberg and his army arrive and save her father's life.

Although Undkan commits some rather cruel acts, he is basically portrayed as a good man. The reader does not have to speculate, for he is told quite frankly that Undkan is a respectable man: "Undkan a bonne mine, & peut inspirer du respect à ceux même qui ne le connoîtroient pas . . ." (21). It is clear that all of

Undkan's acts of cruelty are done under the influence of his evil wife. He allows her to persuade him to require an annual tribute of the neighboring kings, thereby causing war. Furthermore, she maneuvers him into agreeing to Zingis' public execution.

It is because of anger that Abdala decides to put Almanzor and Cleonis to death. Abdala's wife convinces him that they, Almanzor and Cleonis, are lovers. Therefore, believing that he has been betrayed, he gives the order to have them both killed. fortunately, he learns that his wife's suspicions are unfounded, and no harm comes to Almanzor or Almanzaïde.

Generally, the kings in the novels of Anne de la Roche-Guilhen love the hero. In each case, the kings tend to treat him as a son. Amurat devotes much of his attention to rearing Scanderberg; He teaches Scanderberg how to fight and gives him his new Moslem name. Nevertheless, Amurat's love for Scanderberg ends when he discovers that Scanderberg is his rival. Likewise, Abdala loves Almanzor until he believes that Almanzor has deceived him: "Il [Abdala] l'[Almanzor] aima tendrement, & fit toujours une obligeante distinction de luy avec les autres" (5).

Undkan is no exception. He loves Zingis as much as Amurat loves Scanderberg and Abdala loves Almanzor. In fact, Undkan exhibits the greatest love, for he refuses to obey his evil wife for the first time when she tries to get him to humiliate Zingis by requiring him to pay an annual tribute: "Undkan en rejetta la proposition, & par ce qu'il avoit vu faire au Prince des Mongules, il ne croyoit aucunes Puissances capable de le vaincre" (57).

The kings found in Anne de la Roche-Guilhen's novels do not possess many personal character-traits, but they do have some distinguishing ones. The most evident feature of Amurat is his unjustness. One of the narrators in the novel mentions Amurat's unjustness: "Vous n'étes plus un Otage interrompit l'injuste Amurat, mais un Captif dont les Janissaires me rendront conte" (80). The reader makes this discovery when Amurat learns that Scanderberg is one of his rivals; simultaneously, he finds out that Musulman and Mahomet are also his rivals. The only punishment Amurat gives to Musulman and Mahomet is a rather mild reprimand, but he sentences Scanderberg to die. Perhaps Scanderberg's punishment is more severe because Amurat has just heard Arianisse say that she loves Scanderberg. Nevertheless, whatever the reason, Amurat's actions are very inequitable.

In spite of the fact that Undkan supports many evil acts, it is nearly always evident that he is a kindhearted, generous King. The reader is informed, in no uncertain terms, that Undkan's wife is evil. She has an overwhelming power over Undkan and uses it constantly to get him to agree to help carry out her evil plots. Nevertheless, once his wicked wife dies, Undkan is set free—free to be himself: ". . . elle est morte & Undkan delivré de l'esclavage où ses artifices l'avoient mis, rappelle la vertu, qu'elle avoit bannie de son ame & ne respire plus qu'une heureuse reconciliation avec vous [Zingis] . . ." (123-124). In the above quotation, Almundzar is informing Zingis, the young hero, of the death of Undkan's wife and of the fact that Undkan wishes to be reconciled with Zingis. Thus Undkan is free from the horrible influence of the queen and for the first time, the reader sees the true Undkan. It seems that Undkan becomes a new man; he is now the complete opposite of what he appeared to be under the dominance of his spouse.   When he finally gets the opportunity to apologize to Zingis, Undkan's true qualities come to light:

> Oublierez-vous des cruautez, qui me couvrent d'une honte
> eternelle? Seigneur, lui dit Undkan, & pourrez-vous me
> pardonner ce que l'injuste empire, qu'une femme avoit pris
> sur ma foiblesse, m'a fait entreprendre contre vous malgré
> tant de services importants que vous m'avez si généreuse-
> ment rendus? C'est par vos premieres actions que vous
> meritez la Couronne de Tartarie, & tout ce que vous y avez
> ajoûté; & c'est par la vie, que vous m'avez conservée en
> faveur de Taxila, que vous meritez cette Princesse. Je vous
> la donne Zingis, & avec elle la Tartarie. (124-125)

Abdala, the king in *Almanzaïde*, seems to be an archetype who has no real personal character-traits at all. The reader only knows that Abdala loves one of his wives and is dominated by the other. Nevertheless, once it is clear that Abdala is victimized by the domineering queen Roxane, it becomes apparent that Abdala did not want any part of the evil acts he committed. His true character-traits are never clearly described, but he does repent of his evilness as soon as he discovers that Roxane has deceived him:

> . . . le Roy ressentit vivement sa douleur, & le repentir d'avoir écouté les pernicieux advis de Roxane, & que la belle Almanzaïde le vit aux dernieres extremitez de desespoir, Abdemar dont l'amour avoit fait place a une veritable tendresse, s'accusoit seul des malheurs qui estoient arrivez, & se laissant emporter à un veritable repentir, il fit à Roxane des reproches de sa babarie ausquels le Roy joignit les siens. (176-177)

Roxane has convinced Abdala that Almanzor, the young hero, is having an affair with Abdala's wife, and Abdala has given the order to have them both killed. Almanzaïde has just informed the king of the fact that she and Almanzor are Abdala's children. More importantly, Almanzaïde explains that Almanzor is in love with her; he is not in love with Abdala's wife Cleonis. The messenger returns and tells Abdala that he was too late to save Almanzor, and that his wife, Cleonis has been killed. So, when Abdala repents and scolds Roxane, he believes that Almanzor is dead, making this cruel deed inspired by Roxane irreparable. Thus, it is only at the end of the novel, upon witnessing the king's expressions of reget, that the reader meets the true Abdala who is not evil after all.

The Queen

Generally, the queens in the novels of Anne de la Roche-Guilhen are cruel, deceitful and domineering. There is however, one exception. As aforementioned, there are two queens in *Almanzaïde*, and one is depicted as the antithesis of the other:

Roxane is cruel, deceitful and domineering, while Cleonis is kind, helpful and considerate. The only other queen who appears in the three novels under consideration is Zamar, the queen in *Zingis*.

In *Zingis*, the narrator tells us, in no uncertain terms, that Zamar is cruel: ". . . la Cour de Undkan, fut sur le point de servir de theatre [sic] à cruauté de Zamar" (3-4). Throughout the novel, she is seen committing her diabolical acts in order to insure a lucrative future for her cowardly son, Timur. Zamar's cruelty is further evidenced by the fact that she takes pleasure in doing evil, especially when her efforts are successfully carried out. For example, when she has successfully staged the execution of Zingis, she is overjoyed: "Zamar, qui ne voyoit plus sa vengeance differée, goûtoit les félicitez qu'une ame barbare trouve ordinairement dans la cruauté" (114).

Roxane, one of the two queens in *Almanzaïde*, is just as cruel as Zamar—perhaps even more so. Roxane is also very concerned about her son's future and does everything within her power to secure the throne for him; she even poisons Cleonis, the other queen, when she learns that she is with child. Aristan, a slave, informs us that Almanzor and Almanzaïde were born alive only because Cleonis' pregnancy was kept a secret from Roxane: ". . . la cruelle Roxane, ignore qu'elle fust grosse . . ." (88).

Both Zamar and Roxane are quite domineering; they tend to have some mysterious power over their husbands who are extremely afraid of them. Regardless of how evil an act these queens ask their husbands to commit, inevitably, the husbands submit to their wishes. Roxane's dominance extends beyond her spouse. She also tries to rule those around her. When she learns that Almanzaïde is in love with Almanzor instead of with her son, she tells Almanzaïde that she must forget Almanzor and never see him again:

> . . . ie plains de perdre en un mesme iour la veüe de ce precieux Amant, & toutes les espérances que vous pouriez avoir. Retirez-vous, continua-t-elle fierement, allez enfermez vostre honte, & me la cachez comme au reste du

monde. (137-138)

Zamar and Roxane are also very deceitful. In many cases, it is their cunning nature that affords them the opportunity to obtain the desires of their evil hearts. Once Zamar has decided she wants to see Zingis dead, she begins to coerce others into fulfilling her wishes. She chooses judges who agree to cooperate with her by sentencing Zingis to die: "Zamar fit le choix des juges qui condamnerent, suivant ses inspirations, l'illustre Zingis à perdre la tête dans trois jours" (112).

Roxane's deceitfulness is quite visible throughout the novel. When she decides to persuade Abdala, her husband, that Almanzor and Cleonis are having an affair, she pretends to be sad to have to bring him the bad news. This false melancholia is an attempt to appear innocent: "Seigneur, dit-elle à Abdala, en effectant de la tristesse, c'est malgré moy que ie suis contrainte de vous anoncer une chose qui ne vous plaira pas . . ." (151). It seems that she wants her husband to believe that she is as hurt as he by this news. However, she has been searching for a way to get rid of Almanzor, and she is certainly very happy to have found it.

Contrarily, Cleonis is portrayed as the perfect wife. She does not plot against her husband; instead, she does everything within her power to please him. She knows that Roxane has tried to poison her, but instead of exposing her, Cleonis bears her child, feigns his death and sends him away from the palace. Obviously, she realizes that Roxane is a formidable foe who would stop at nothing to secure the throne for her own son. On another occasion, Cleonis exemplifies her kindheartedness and concern for others by warning Almanzor of the fact that Abdemar is his rival, and that he and Roxane are trying to find a way to get him permanently banished from the country:

> . . . Almanzor . . . il faut que ie vous donne un avis qui vous est important, puisque ce moment permet de vous parler sans témoins, vous aimez Almanzaïde, Abdemar est vostre Rival, & prétend pour vous éloigner pour iamais,

vous faire affranchir par le Roy & sortir non seulement de ce Palais, mais de Moroc. (118-119)

Roxane's and Zamar's evilness stems from their ambitiousness and their love for their respective sons. They appear to have their son's best interests at heart, but they always choose evil tactics in order to secure the goal they have set for them. These queens seem to be somewhat unselfish, for nearly everything that they do is an effort to establish a lucrative, trouble-free future for their sons. Aparently, neither Roxane nor Zamar trusts fate; furthermore, neither trusts her husband's or her son's ability. Roxane and Zamar would go to any length necessary to establish a royal inheritance for their sons—they will even kill to do so (Roxane tries to kill Cleonis, and Zamar attempts to have Zingis executed).

When grouped in their respective categories—heroes, heroines, kings, queens—the characters of Anne de la Roche-Guilhen have many similarities. The heroes are generally brave, gallant and madly in love while the heroines are kind, gentle and loving; the kings are usually weak cowards, and the queens are basically strong, manipulative monsters. Nevertheless, there is a restrictive factor in the life of each of these characters, and it mainly controls the manner in which they conduct themselves. In the case of the hero, it is the fact that he is in love. It seems that everything he does is based on his love for the heroine. In many cases, the hero goes off to war only to prove himself worthy of his beloved. He is veritably blinded by love and therefore often endangers his life without the slightest hesitation.

Although she is portrayed as an innocent young princess, the heroine has a strong desire to be free to live as she chooses. The flames of this desire are often fed by her love for the hero. There is invariably someone who is openly against her choice of suitor, and even if this particular person happens to be her father, the heroine refuses to obey him.

The kings are generally controlled by fear. They all tend to be afraid of their wives. Nevertheless, once the queens are observed in action, it becomes clear that the kings have a right to be afraid for the queens, who will do whatever it takes to assure their sons' happiness, are fierce demons, driven by motherly passion.

One of the most intriguing and unique aspects of Anne de la Roche-Guilhen's treatment of characterization, however, is the manner in which her heroes and heroines are placed in an inescapable prison and held there throughout the novel by the villainous adversary, love. As previously mentioned, la Roche-Guilhen's main characters become the victims of Cupid's un-avoidable arrow even from the beginning of the novel. Once love-stricken, the heroes and heroines are rendered helpless, and though they devote all of their efforts to finding a means of escape from the many heartaches love brings, they find none. It is only after the arrival of a force stronger than any man, *the deus ex machina*, that la Roche-Guilhen's characters are set free to get married.

The heroes of Anne de la Roche-Guilhen all seem to be helpless when confronted with the insurmountable power of love. Immediately upon meeting their beloved, they are captivated. Their thoughts and their desires change; they no longer seek glory for themselves, and their personal aspirations are quickly forgotten. In short, once they have been enslaved by love, la Roche-Guilhen's heroes appear to be reborn; they are possessed by a force they have never known before.

Perhaps Anne de la Roche-Guilhen was influenced by the courtly love that appeared in French literature during previous centuries, for once her hero has been captivated by the beauty of some princess, he immediately becomes obsessed with the idea of proving himself worthy of her. Everything he does thereafter is an effort to please his newly-found beloved. Completely submitted to the heroine, the hero goes off to do battle, fights in duels, and generally endangers his life to prove his love for the princess. Nonetheless, whereas the invincible warrior of medieval French literature finds joy in serving his beloved, la Roche-Guilhen's hero is deeply saddened by the many obstacles that stand between him and the princess with whom he is enamored.

Almanzor, the hero in *Almanzaïde*, falls in love with Alman-zaïde during their youth. Suddenly, his love for her becomes so strong that he proclaims that he would rather die than live without her. Even after he learns that Almanzaïde is his sister, Almanzor's love for her does not change: "Almanzor, qui sous le nom d'amant & de frere, prenoit toujours également du plaisir à la regarder" (102).

Contrary to the means by which Almanzor falls in love, the hero in *Le Grand Scanderberg* is seduced upon hearing the beautiful voice of Arianisse. Though he has not seen her face, Scanderberg is instantaneously imprisoned by love: "Le son de cette voix frapa mes oreilles d'une maniére [sic] qui passa jusques à mon coeur" (23). Thus, at this point in the novel, this invincible soldier, one who wins all battles, is rendered powerless.

The hero in *Zingis* has his first encounter with love when he enters a garden forbidden to men. Upon his arrival in Undkan's court Zingis is tired from his trip, so he goes into a garden to rest. He is not aware of the fact that trouble awaits him there. When he enters the garden, Timur attacks Zingis—an attempt to chase him out of the garden—and more importantly, Zingis sees Taxila for the first time. Zingis ". . . qui ne pouvoit detourner ses yeux d'un objet si charmant, sentoit déja [sic] les puissantes impressions que sa beaute extraordinaire faisoit sur lui" (23).

Likewise, the heroines in the novels of Anne de la Roche-Guilhen are caught in the inescapable web of love. They are not only the prisoners of love, but they are also portrayed as the captives of some king or ambitious prince. Almanzaïde, who is actually the king's daughter, is given to the evil Roxane as a slave. Arianisse, the heroine in *Le Grand Scanderberg*, is king Amurat's captive. He is in love with her, but Arianisse hates him. Unlike Almanzaïde and Arianisse, Taxila is not physically a slave, but she is imprisoned emotionally. Taxila has been promised, by her father, to the cowardly Timur, whom she hates.

As one observes la Roche-Guilhen's treatment of love in relation to characterization, it is quite clear that her novels reflect the ideas of great men of the seventeenth century such as Pascal. Pascal's thoughts are based on the Jansenist belief—predestinations: man is incapable of good; those who have not received the grace of God, which is given to those whom God chooses, are condemned to do evil. In accordance with the beliefs of the Jansenists, the antagonists, especially Roxane and Zamar, are seeminly compelled to do evil because of the lack of God's grace. As these demon-like queens are observed comnmitting their wicked acts, it becomes apparent that they do not possess the power to change their ways.

Contrarily, the two kings, Abdala and Undkan, who submit themselves to carrying out the malicious schemes of their wives repent and find forgiveness for their sins—hence Christian beliefs: "If we confess our sins, he [God] is faithful and just to forgive us our sins, and to cleanse us from all unrighteousness" (1 John 1.9.). After Zamar's death—just punishment according to the ideology of the Greek tragedy—Undkan begs Zingis to forgive him. Zingis graciously forgives him; thus Undkan is able to live a happy, peaceful life. When Abdala learns that he has been duped by his evil wife, Roxane, he repents of his many transgressions against Almanzor, his own son: ". . . le Roy ressentit vivement sa douleur, & le repentir d'avoir écouté les pernicieux advis de Roxane . . ." (176).

The treatment of characterization in Anne de la Roche-Guilhen's novels is quite different from that of other seventeenth-century novelists. La Calprenède's ". . . heroes and heroines . . . [are] mere idealizations of the lords and ladies he had met in the salons of Paris" (Kastner and Atkins 125). The hero of Gomberville is so busy wandering from place to place that his romantic attachments seem rather distant. Madeleine de Scudéry depicts real people of her day by adding ". . . allusions to and portraits of the men and women of the precieux society . . ." (Kastner and Atkins 125). The personnages of La Calprenède, Gomberville and Mlle de Scudéry do not possess the same passion that is seen in the heroes and heroines of Anne de la Roche-Guilhen, a Huguenot refugee. La Roche-Guilhen's characters are driven by an uncontrolled passion which inevitably leads to melancholy. La Roche-Guilhen's characters are unique in that they are not mere imitations of the seventeenth-century "lords and ladies", but they represent the universal struggle of mankind.

With a careful examination of la Roche-Guilhen's heroes and heroines, it is quite apparent that she made a very important contribution to the development of the French novel. Her works foreshadow a philosophy that was adopted by twentieth-century existentialist novelists—existence, confrontation with others and with God, is tragic. As la Roche-Guilhen's heroes and heroines are unrolled, it becomes clear that their existence is indeed tragic. Having been struck by Cupid's arrow, they are forced to abide in a living hell. Like the characters of Jean-Paul Sartre in *Huis clos*, la Roche-Guilhen's personnages find that being in the presence of their beloved is torment itself. Nevertheless, there is no means of escape. Although the heroes are tortured by the presence of the heroines, they are unable to find happiness without them.

Trapped in the unavoidable web of love, seemingly doomed forever, la Roche-Guilhen's hero does not give up. Like Sisyphus —*Le Mythe de Sisyphe* by Albert Camus—whom the gods had condemned to ceaselessly rolling a rock to the top of a mountain whence the stone would fall back of its own weight, la Roche-Guilhen's hero never stops trying to find happiness with his beloved. Nonetheless, his efforts are futile, for he is helpless. Unlike the twentieth-century novelists, Anne de la Roche-Guilhen- —a romantic at heart—obviously was unable to keep her characters in limbo. Overwhelmed by the imprisonment of her loving creations, she calls upon the *deus ex machina* who sets them free.

Chapter Four

The Narrative Style of
Anne de la Roche-Guilhen

A novelist may choose to employ one or a combination of several types of narration: omniscient narrator, narrator-agent, view-point character, dialogue, letter, journal. Quite often, a combination of narrative techniques is used; but in modern French novels, as well as in those of other nations, it is not rare to find a single form of narration throughout. There are advantages and disadvantages of using one or several narrative techniques. When a single narrative device is used, the work is likely to have a coherance of tone. In this case, if the novel is artfully written, the reader is apt to readily accept the narrator's point of view, for he has nothing else with which to compare it. On the other hand, if different narrative devices are employed, there are constant interruptions, and the reader is exposed to several points of view—that of the narrator and maybe of the characters themselves.

The omniscient narrator who is " . . . the actual author and real teller of the fiction . . . is, of course, omniscient, omnipotent, and omnipresent" (Macauley and Lanning 111). Unlike the narrator-agent or the viewpoint character, he ". . . is not bound by time, space, or circumstance" (Foster-Harris 40). The omniscient narrator is actually the creator of the characters; therefore, he even knows their innermost thoughts. He not only knows what they have done in the past, are doing presently, and will do in the future, but he can also perceive how they would act in any given situation. In *Technique in Fiction,* Robie Macauley and George Lanning give a very useful summary of the capabilities of the omniscient narrator:

> [1] He can make selective use of a number of individual points of view, borrowing a specific character's angle of vision when it suits his purpose. [2] He can use the theatre of "showing not telling," for the moment presenting a quite objective look at things. [3] He can take a panoramic view of events, giving an account of simultaneous happenings or disassociated scenes that a narrator-agent could cover only by use of most improbable devices. [5] He can discover multiple traits and facets of the characters readily and plausibly without having to work things around to bring any single point of view within discovery range. (111-112)

The narrator-agent differs from the omniscient narrator in that he is not the author himself. Actually, the narrator-agent" . . . is the author's point of view (transformed either in small ways or in large), personified and humanized" (Macauley and Lanning 104). The narrator-agent may be thought of as the author's hired worker. He is called upon when the author does not wish to narrate his story. He is the over-seer of the author's creations, the characters. The narrator-agent follows the authors's personages from place to place, observing their actions and reactions to others and reports to the reader what he sees, hears and suspects. He does not have any way of knowing the characters' inner thoughts, but since he is often allowed to interpret what he sees and hears, he may attempt to guess what is going on in the minds of the characters. Much like the author, the narrator-agent is able to give a panoramic view of the story, for he can move about freely, spying on any person-age at any time he chooses. In spite of all the freedom and power the narrator-agent is given, he is not allowed to interact with the characters he has under surveillance, asking and answering questions, for as soon as he is given an active role in the story he is no longer a narrator-agent, but he becomes a view-point character.

The view-point character is an active participant in the story. He may be one of the main actors or one of the minor ones. Moreover, the view-point character is obviously never omniscient, omnipotent or omnipresent. He has no more power than the other actors. He does not know everything; he is not all-powerful; he cannot be present everywhere. In fact, the view-point character only knows what he sees, overhears or is told. Basically, all other personages in the story are simply objects outside the view-point character. Thus, the view-point character is assigned the task of describing the other actors from the outside—he does not know their inner thoughts. Furthermore, he is not able to give a panoramic view of the story.

In addition to the omniscient narrator, the narrator-agent, and the view-point character, novelists have many other devices of narration, such as the dialogue, letter, or journal at their disposal. The letter is a very effectual narrative technique when used properly. Quite often, the letters that one finds in literary works are written by one lover to another. It is a useful instrument to show what has transpired in the meanwhile—it takes the reader to another setting, and frequently to another time; it informs the reader, as well as the actor who receives it, of the sender's feelings, or it brings a word of warning to its recipient. Regardless of its main messages, if skillfully employed by the author, the letter accomplishes many goals. When the letter is intercepted by an enemy, as is often the case in the works of Anne de la Roche-Guilhen, it adds yet another complication to the plot. Thus, the epistolary technique is such an intriguing narrative device that some authors, such as Montesquieu *(Lettres persanes)*, were inspired to write novels composed entirely of letters.

The dialogue is a narrative technique that has enjoyed a perpetual existence. This device is used to give the narrator—whether omniscient, narrator-agent or view-point character—a break from the task of telling the story. At this point, the narrator allows his characters to speak for themselves. Thus, the reader is given the opportunity to observe the personages as they act and react with each other and listen secretly to their private conversations. When the dialogue is employed, the distance between the reader and the actors is lessened. The reader no longer has to rely on a narrator, who inevitably gives his own point of view; the reader collects his information on a first-hand basis.

In the modern French novel such as Sartre's *La Nausée* and Bernanos' *Journal d'un curé de campagne*, for example, another narrative device, the journal, is used. Usually a view-point character is presented as the writer of a journal (diary). The main difference between the regular view-point character and the one who writes a journal is that the latter makes a written re-port—sometimes giving the dates of each entry—of what he sees and hears while the regular view-point character simply tells what he knows to the reader.

Regardless of the narrative technique an author chooses, he may present his narrator by utilizing either first, second, or third-person narration (the plural persons such as "we" and "they" are generally unacceptable in fiction). "The reader's sympathies and identification are likely to be given to the narrator who has a role in the story, and this is somewhat truer of the first person than of the person teller" (Macauley and Lanning 109). When the third-person point of view is employed, it appears that the reader is farther removed from the story than when the first person point of view is utilized. Hearing the "I" repeated continuously, the reader is apt to feel that someone close by is telling the story. Nevertheless, if skillfully plied, second-person narration is as effective as the first person.

Omniscient Narrator

In the works of Anne de la Roche-Guilhen, it is the omniscient narrator and view-point character who tell the story. La Roche-Guilhen, like many other writers, used a combination of narrative techniques. In her novels, the omniscient narrator ties together the narratives of the various view-point characters.   First, the omniscient narrator sets the scene for the entire novel, then he disappears—only returning when needed to bid one of the view-point characters farewell and introduce another; finally he returns to give a fairytale ending—the hero and heroine live happily ever after.

In the novels of Anne de la Roche-Guilhen, the view-point character usually plays a very active role.   Sometimes he is even the hero himself.   This particular narrative device is called upon, in la Roche-Guilhen's works, when one character sets out to tell his story to another.   As aforementioned, this novelistic convention—allowing one character to tell his story to another—recurs throughout the novels of la Roche-Guilhen.   In fact, the view-point character is utilized more often in her works than any other narrative device.

It is the omniscient narrator who is in charge of narration at the very beginning of la Roche-Guilhen's novels.   He usually commences by setting the scene—giving the name of the country in which the action takes place, the name of the ruling king and a short description of him.   At the beginning of *Almanzaïde*, the reader is told by the omniscient narrator that the action takes place in Maroc and that the king is a just man who has brought peace to this African nation:

> Le Royaume de Maroc ayant été long-temps dechiré par des resolutions fascheuses, & oppressé par des dominations tiraniques, tomba sous celle d'Abdala, le plus juste, le mieux faisant, & le plus vertueux de tous les Princes; il donna ses premières années aux armes avec succez, & s'estant acquis une glorieuse reputation, il s'assura un repos tranquille dans la plus fameuse Ville de l'Afrique. (1-2)

The omniscient narrator in *Le Grand Scanderberg* starts his narration with the sanctification of Scanderberg, the hero. Nothing is said about the setting until the greatness of Scanderberg's character is expounded upon: "La valeur & générosité n'ont jamais

paru avec tant d'èclat, qu'en la personne de l'invincible Scanderberg . . . & sa vertu peut servir d'exemple à tous les Souverains
du Monde" (5). The omniscient narrator in *Zingis*, like the one in
Almanzaïde, begins the novel by setting the scene and describing
the character of the king. Nevertheless, the character of Undkan,
the king in *Zingis*, contrasts that of Abdala, the king of *Almanzaïde*. Whereas Abdala is a good leader, Undkan is a weakling
who brings tyranny to the throne:

> La Tartarie Orientale aprés avoir eu plusieurs Rois dignes
> de gouverner cette belle partie du monde, se vit dans la
> suite des tems soumise à Undkan Prince foible & possedé
> par une épouse imperieuse, qui ne lui inspiroit que des
> violences. (3)

The action in *Zingis* begins, *in medias res*, on page five.
Suddenly, the omniscient narrator plunges his reader into the
heroine's bedroom. Just as the reader is surprised by the abrupt
entry into her room, Taxila, the heroine, is surprised by the
sudden intrusion of her angry father:

> Une nuit que Taxila étoit occupé du souvenir de Zingis, elle
> entendit un grand bruit, & vit entrer le roi son pere dans sa
> chambre, qui venoit, les yeux pleins de fureur, lui repro-
> cher une secréte intelligence avec son plus mortel ennemi
> [Zingis]. (5)

The omniscient narrator clarifies this mystery by choosing one
of the guards to explain the king's anger to Taxila. Zingis has just
been captured trying to enter the palace; thus, the king suspects his
daughter, Taxila, of willfully taking part in the secret plot: "Un
Officier des Gardes lui expliqua ce mystere, en lui apprenant que
Zingis venoit d'être supris à une des portes du palais . . . " (5-6).
    In the novels of Anne de la Roche-Guilhen, the omniscient
narrator also takes it upon himself to end the novel. All of la
Roche-Guilhen's novels, though quite different throughout, have

a fairy-tale ending—the prince and the princess live happily ever after. The omniscient narrator ends *Almanzaïde* with: "[Almanzor] goûta avec elle [Almanzaïde] toutes les douceurs d'une vie longue, glorieuse & tranquille, apres avoir rendu son nom fameux par toute l'Afrique" (225-226). The omniscient narrator's last words in *Le Grand Scanderberg* are:

> Jamais Roi ne vecut plus content, & ne fit d'actions si fameuses que Scanderberg; mais suffit ici de l'avoir lié pour jamais avec la chére Arianisse: & les grands evenements de son Reyne etant connus, il seroit inutile de les redire. (178)

After a long enumeration of what happens in the end, the omniscient narrator in *Zingis* ends with " . . . & ces Princes, comblez d'honneurs & de jours, laisserent une ample & glorieuse posterité" (160).

Another function of the omniscient narrator in Anne de la Roche-Guilhen's works is the tying together of the various stories told by the view-point characters. This narrative responsibility, however, is shared by the view-point characters. Frequently, the view-point character informs the reader of an impending story to be told by a certain personage; occasionally, it is in a dialogue that this discovery is made. Most often, it is the omniscient narrator who assumes the responsibility of introducing a story which is to be told by a view-point character. Since the omniscient narrator is able to give a panoramic view of the entire novel, in many cases, he is better equipped to tie together the various stories found in la Roche-Guilhen's works.

The omniscient narrator's role of tying together stories is apparent in each of the three novels that are analyzed in this study. In *Almanzaïde*, when Aristan notices Almanzor's extremely sad state of mind, he begins to question him in order to learn the cause. At first, Almanzor tries to avoid his question, but finally he tells Aristan that he is in love with Almanzaïde—hence the cause of his melancholy. Almanzor mistakes the look on Aristan's face to mean that Aristan is interested in hearing the complete story. So, he tells it to him. Later, the reader learns that this was actually a look of disbelief on Aristan's face, for he knew that Almanzor and Almanzaïde were sister and brother. Thus, the omniscient narrator interrupts this conversation to inform the reader that Almanzor is about to tell his and Almanzaïde's story: "L'Enuque [Aristan] ne fit que porter ces yeux vers le Ciel, & Almanzor continua de cette sorte" (20). The omniscient narrator indicates the ending of Almanzor's story by abruptly stating that: "Almanzor finit là son récit . . ." (64).

Fifty pages later, Almanzor ends his story which explains how he and Almanzaïde fell in love. Understanding the seriousness of their love, Aristan decides to tell Almanzor that Almanzaïde is his sister. Almanzor is devastated: "Almanzor estoit immobile à son tour, il ne fut iamais de douleur comparable à la sienne, il detesta sa destinée, & demeura un accablement déplorable . . ." (70). It is at this point that Aristan attempts to clarify this terrible truth by explaining the mysterious births of Almanzor and Almanzaïde. The omniscient narrator steps in to emphasize the fact that Aristan is about to tell this particular story to Almanzor: ". . . Aristan lui apprit de cette sorte le mystere de sa Naissance" (70).

Once *Le Grand Scanderberg* has begun *in medias res*, and Scanderberg returns to the castle with his friends, Thopia expresses his desire to hear how Scanderberg happened to fall in love with Arianisse. "Thopia scavoit bien que Scanderberg etoit, Amoureux; mais il ignoroit les particularitez de sa vie, & temoigna une forte envie d'en être informé" (13). Of course Scanderberg is obliged to share this dramatic event with him, so he clears the room and sets out to tell his story. The omniscient narrator sets the stage for Scanderberg's story by stating that: "Scanderberg ordonna qu'on les laissat seuls, & commenca son discours en ces termes" (14). At this point the omniscient narrator relinquishes the job of narration to the view-point character, Scanderberg, but the omniscient narrator returns seventy-five pages later to inform the reader that Scanderberg's story has ended: "Le Roi d'Albanie cessa de parler, & soupira d'une maniere si touchante, que Thopia, qui l'aimoit veritablement, en fut émû jusques au fond de l'ame"

(89).

Subsequently, after his emotional reaction to Scanderberg's story, Thopia explains to Scanderberg that he understands how he feels, for he too has been struck by Cupid's merciless arrow. Scanderberg does not believe that Thopa has experienced the effects of love, nor does he believe that Thopia understands what he feels: "Vous ne connoissez point l'amour mon cher Thopia . . . & vous ne pouvez comprendre ce que je sens" (113). Orane quickly suggests that Scanderberg allow Thopia to tell his story:

> Seigneur, interrompit Orane, qui ne cherchoit qu'à distraire
> son Maître de ses tristes pensées; pour convaincre le roi de
> cette verité apprenez-lui vos avantures amoureuses. Oüi,
> Thopia, ajoûta Scanderberg; je vous écouterai avec atten-
> tion, quelque préoccupé que je sois . . . & vous en allez
> être persuadé, par le recit que vous m'ordonnez de vous
> faire. (114)

Immediately, Thopia begins his story. Thus, Thopia, who is now the view-point character, becomes the narrator; the omniscient narrator returns to say that: "Scanderberg embrassa Thopia, quand il eut cessé de parler, & l'assura qu'Amisse seroit à lui . . ." (141).

The next story in *Le Grand Scanderberg* is narrated by Arianisse. With regard to all three novels under consideration (*Almanzaïde*, *Le Grand Scanderberg* and *Zingis*), this is the first and only time a female character is given the opportunity to tell a story to men. One evening when Arianisse is alone with Scander-berg, Thopia and Amisse, she finds it necessary to explain to Scanderberg what happened to her during her absence from him. The omniscient narrator indicates that: "Arianisse . . . voulut satisfaire la curiosité de Scanderberg; & étant un soir avec Amisse & Thopia, qui sçavoient ses premières avantures, elle apprit les dernières au Roi d'Albanie [Scanderberg] en ces termes" (156). As Arianisse's story ends, the omniscient narrator dutifully makes it clear that she is no longer the narrator: "La Princesse cessa de parler; & Scanderberg lui fit connoître une partie des mouvemens, que sons recit lui avoit inspirez par les différentes souffrances où elle avoit été exposée" (175).

In *Zingis*, Once Zerbin has finished the story of Zingis and Taxila, the omniscient narrator assumes the role of narrator. Zerbin tells this story to Philing who is not only interested in the life of a great man such as Zingis but is also willing, after hearing the story, to risk his life to help set Zingis free from prison. When Zerbin ends the story, the omniscient narrator utters his usual words: "Zerbin cessa de parler . . ." (70). As soon as Philing's curiosity concerning Zingis has been satisfied, Almundzar is very impatient to hear about Philing's many adventures. The omniscient narrator introduces Philing's story by stating that: "Almunzar, qui avoit beaucoup d'envie de sçavoir les avantures de Philing, le pria de ne lui retarder pas ce plaisir; & le roi de Tibet, qui ne pouvoir être occupé plus agreablement qu'en parlant d'axione, reprit ainsi la parole" (79). As Philing ends his story, the omniscient narrator intervenes with: "Philing cesssa de parler . . ." (108). Just when it seems that the novel will end, all of the characters express a desire to hear the story of Omir and Thamirize (minor characters). The omniscient narrator appears once again to introduce Omir's story. He indicates that: "Tout le monde ayant envie d'apprendre par quelle fortune Omir & Thamirize étoient ensemble, le Prince de Brema [Omir] avec la permission de la Princesse, parla de cette sorte à ces Illustres personnes" (128).

In the novels of Anne de la Roche-Guilhen, it is also the omniscient narrator who reveals the letters that are written to and by the various personages. This, however, is another responsibility that is shared with the view-point character. It is only in *Almanzaïde* and *Le Grand Scanderberg*, and not in *Zingis*, that the omniscient narrator serves in this capacity. While disclosing the letter from Cleonis to Almanzor, the omsicient narrator begins by explaining that since Cleonis " . . . ne pouvoit chercher Almanzor elle mesme . . . elle lui écrivit un Billet qu'elle donna à un vieil Enuque pour lui porter . . ." (144). With the intervention of the omniscient narrator, the reader learns why Cleonis writes this letter and how she had it delivered to Almanzor. Immediately thereafter, the omniscient narrator adds words that make it quite clear that he intends to share the exact words of this letter with the reader: " . . . il y avoit ce peu de mots" (144). This letter inevitably causes much chaos: "Que cet innocent Billet causa de trouble dans le Palais d'Abdala . . ." (146).

In la Roche-Guilhen's works, the omniscient narrator even criticizes the disposition of the various personages—especially that of the evil queens. The omniscient narrator makes judgemental comments about Roxane, the evil queen in *Almanzaïde*, such as: " . . . l'esprit de Roxane estoit naturellement mechant . . ." (148). He criticizes Zamar, the evil queen in *Zingis*, with descriptions like "cruelle Zamar" (111). Some of the other judgements of character are more subtle. For example, referring to Zamar, the omniscient narrator simply states that "Zamar goutoit le plaisir d'être maîtresse de la destinée d'un homme qui avoit tant fait souffrir sa fierté" (8).

View-Point Character

Throughout the novels of Anne de la Roche-Guilhen, the view-point character tells his or someone else's life story. This narrative device involves one of the characters, usually one of the main ones, who for some particular reason tells a story to another personage in order to explain what has happened before the action of the novel begins. Quite often, in the works of Anne de la Roche-Guilhen, the view-point character is forced or at least encouraged by another personage to tell his story.

In *Almanzaïde*, the first story is given the title "Histoire d'Almanzor et d'Almanzaïde". This story is told by Almanzor, now a view-point character, who speaks to Aristan. Almanzor tells his story to explain how he fell in love with Almanzaïde and thus clarifies the cause of his (Almanzor's) melancholy. Since he is telling his story to Aristan, who knows Almanzaïde well, but is not aware of the love between her and Almanzor, Almanzor begins by pointing out that he will not give a physical description of Almanzaïde: "Il n'est pas necessaire que ie vous fasse le portrait d'Almanzaïde, elle vous est connue . . ." (21).

Once Almanzor finishes his story, Aristan informs Almanzor that he and Almanzaïde are sister and brother and cannot be lovers. Almanzor is completely overwhelmed. In an effort to clarify this matter, Aristan tells the "Histoire de la Naissance d'Almanzor et d'Almanzaïde".

The view-point character also plays the role of story teller in *Le Grand Scanderberg*. The first view-point character to assume this role is Scanderberg himself. At the beginning of the novel, Thopia is aware that Scanderberg is in love, but he knows none of the details. So, in order to reveal what has happened before, Scanderberg tells his story: "Histoire de Scanderberg". After listening to Scanderberg's entire story, Thopia shares his story: "Histoire de Thopia". Finally, in order to give an explanation of what happened to her while separated from Scanderberg, Arianisse tells her story: "Histoire d'Arianisse." Arianisse's story appears near the end of the novel, and it is relatively short when compared to Thopia's and Scanderberg's stories. Arianisse narrates only eighteen pages while Thopia's story requires twenty-six pages and Scanderberg's a remarkable seventy-five pages.

Zerbin, a minor character, is the first to act as view-point character in *Zingis*. Zerbin tells the "Histoire de Zingis & de la Princesse Taxila" to Philing, a visiting king who admires Zingis and who wishes to help set him free. Zerbin's story is different from the others in that he does not tell his own story, but that of Zingis and Taxila. Thus, Zerbin does not play an active role in this story; instead, he is an observer. Consequently, Zerbin seems to play the role of a narrator-agent, for he can only tell Philing what he has seen, heard or been told. Whereas other view-point characters—telling their own story—use first-person narration, Zerbin is forced to use third-person narration.

Once he has heard Zingis' story in its entirety, Philing is obliged to tell his story. Philing tells his story to Almunzar, a king who has recently befriended him and who has instructed

Zerbin to tell Zingis' story to Philing. Philing's story is given the title: "Histoire de Philing & d'Axione". Finally, Omir who is a minor personage comes forward as view-point character, and tells the "Histoire d'Omir & de Thamirize".

In the novels of Anne de la Roche-Guilhen, with advance warning of the change from one narrator to another, the reader is not easily confused by the use of the different narrators. In many cases, the view-point character's story is so long that one could possibly forget who the narrator is before arriving at the end of the story. However, to make sure that this does not happen, the view-point character in la Roch-Guilhen's novels constantly reminds the reader that he, the view-point character, is speaking to a certain persona. This feat is accomplished by the view-point character's constant reference to his listener (often by name), seemingly in an effort to maintain his undivided attention. This narrative device is not very prevalent in *Almanzaïde*, but it appears throughout *Le Grand Scanderberg* and quite often in *Zingis*. As Scanderberg tells his story to Thopia he refers to Thopia by name on several occasions: "Enfin, Thopia, le moment du combat arriva . . ." (21); "Je rougis, Thopia, en vous redisant les douceurs de Selimane . . ." (26); "Voilà, Thopia, dans quelle état nous vimes la Cour . . ." (32); "Jugez, mon cher Thopia; quelle fut ma douleur . . ." (45); ". . . mais Thopia, ce n'étoit pas ces Riveaux que j'avois à craindre . . ." (71). The above quotations are simply a sampling of Scanderberg's many references to Thopia.

Although Thopia and Arianisse, while telling their stories, do not refer to Scanderberg by name, they make reference to him on several occasions. Usually, Scanderberg is respectfully referred to as "Seigneur". While telling his story, Thopia makes statements such as: "Ce fut alors, Seigneur, que toute la terre parla de vous avec admiration . . ." (126); "Mais Seigneur, c'est ici le lieu de vous parler de mes chagrins" (127); "Mais, Seigneur, il est temps de vous dire quelque chose de plus remarquable" (164). Likewise, as she narrates her story, Arianisse makes references such as: "Enfin, Seigneur, on apprit à Andrinople votre entrée dans Croie . . ." (169); "Enfin, Seigneur, nous partimes du Serrail d'Andrinople" (171).

In *Zingis*, as mentioned above, the view-point character makes fewer references to his listener than the view-point characters in *Le Grand Scanderberg*. As Philing tells his story to Almundzar, he refers to his listener on several occasions: "Je vous avouë, Almundzar, que je sentis de l'amour dés ce moment" (83); ". . . mais, Almundzar, quand sa taille eut formée . . ." (87-88); "Enfin, Almundzar, sans m'arreter à Kachen, je parcourus tout le Tibet . . ." (106).

Dialogue

The dialogue is another narrative device used in the novels of Anne de la Roche-Guilhen. This novelistic convention affords the reader an opportunity to witness the verbal interaction of the characters. Plied skillfully, the dialogue narrows the distance between the personages and the reader. La Roche-Guilhen's dialogues are quite skillfully done, but the constant interruptions by the narrator or view-point character remind the reader that the story is being told to him—hence, the distance is re-established and the dramatic effect is lost. In *Almanzaïde*, after telling his story, Almanzor interrogates Aristan and discovers that Almanzaïde, the princess he loves, is in reality his sister:

> ne me parlerez-vous point? luy dit-il, . . . Ha! Almanzor, reprit l'Enuque, vous ne les sçavez pas tous . . . Comment, interrompit Almanzor, tout émeu . . . quel repentir doivent suive les sentimens que i'ay pour la plus belle . . . personne du monde. Je sçay bien, repliqua l'Enuque, que sa beauté . . . & sa vertu vous rendent excusable . . . mais Almanzor, apprenez, puis qu'il faut vous le dire, qu'elle est vostre soeur . . . Ma soeur! s'écria douloureusement, Almanzor, Ha! ne m'abusez point [;] j'en mourrois, Arristan . . . (64-68)

The dialogue between Almanzor and Aristan does not end there;

nevertheless, the above quotation is a sufficient representation of the dialogue in Mlle de la Roche-Guilhen's works, for the dialogues in *Le Grand Scanderberg* and *Zingis* are the same from a stylistic point of view. In both Scanderberg and Zingis, the dialogues are encumbered with words like: "lui dit-il," "s'écria-t-il," "ajoûta-t-il," "dit-elle," "répondit le Tartare."

Furthermore, in la Roche-Guilhen's works, the view-point character, though his domain is not as vast as that of the omniscient narrator, takes the liberty of quoting the personages about whom he is telling the story. Realizing that the view-point character can only report what he sees, hears or suspects, it seems impossible and it is improbable that he would be able to remember the exact words of a conversation he heard years before. Nonetheless, the view-point characters in Mlle de la Roche-Guilhen's novels, without any explanation of how they are able to do so, cite conversations repeatedly. While telling his story to Thopia, Scanderberg quotes a previous conversation between Arianisse and himself:

> Allez, Seigneur, me dit-elle tristement, allez en Albanie; vangez vôtre Sang, delivrez de grandes Princesses qui ne peuvent espérer qu'en vous; prenez possession du Trone de Castriot; protegez Aranit, & n'oubliez pas Arianisse. Si vous vouliez, repris-je, je ne fuirois pas seul. Hélas! Seigneur, repliqua-t-elle, je vous suivrois sans repugnance, si vous étiez en état de me retirer d'ici. (86)

It is not likely that Scanderberg was able to remember Arianisse's and his exact words. It is even more improbable that Philing, a character in *Zingis*, was capable of recalling a conversation he did not hear. Philing even admits that he was not in the palace when this conversation between Hildezar and Philing's beloved Axione took place:

> Un jour que je n'étois point dans le Palais, Hildezar trouva Axione qui se promenoit seule sur une terrasse . . . Arre-

tez, Axione, qui m'en prevoyoit point, sourit à ces paroles.
De quoi? Seigneur, reprit-elle, est-ce des obligations que je
vous ai, & me voulez-vous reprocher d'avoir manqué à
quelque chose de ce que je leur dois? Si vous m'aviez de
l'obligation, répondit Hildezar, il seroit facile de vous en
acquitter . . . (89)

Thus, the plausibility of the dialogue included in la Roche-
Guilhen's view-point character's stories, to say the least, is
questionable.

Letter

Anne de la Roche-Guilhen also used the letter as a narrative
device. As mentioned above, the letter is a novelistic convention
that may be employed to convey action that takes place at another
time or in another place, to warn a particular personage about a
certain matter, or simply to bring good or bad news to its recipient. In most cases, in la Roche-Guilhen's novels, these letters are
included in the text in their entirety. The reader is offered no
explanation of how the narrator, especially the view-point character, is able to share the contents of these letters with his listener.
Nevertheless, la Roche-Guilhen only includes one letter in
Almanzaïde—not counting the letter that is mentioned near the end
of the novel. The stranger arrives proclaiming that Almanzaïde is
in reality the princess of Fez; he is carrying a letter to prove it.
The contents of this letter are not shared with the reader. When
Cleonis learns about Roxane's plot to have Almanzor banished
from the country, however, she decides to tell him about it. So,
she writes him a letter to arrange a meeting:

Il est important que ie vous revoye aujourd'hui, ayant des
choses à vous apprendre que je ne peux confier à papier,
Trouvez-vous dans deux heures à la fontaine du Labirinte,
ie ne manqueray pas de m'y rendre, & de vous faire
connoistre si vos interests me sont chers, & quels sentimens

a pour vous. (145-146)

Unfortunately this letter falls into the hands of the evil Roxane who immediately concludes that Cleonis and Almanzor are lovers. Considering what Cleonis does not say in this letter, one could easily be persuaded that she and Almanzor are indeed intimately involved. Roxane has very little trouble convincing the king that Cleonis and Almanzor are lovers. Thus, it appears, at least for a while, that Roxane's diabolical plot to get rid of Almanzor will succeed. But in the end, justice prevails.

In *Le Grand Scanderberg*, the contents of five letters are revealed. There is such a large number of letters in *Le Grand Scanderberg* because two of them are written in response to two others. The first letter deals with an order from the king, whereas the remaining four concern lovers. While searching the body of Aradin, Thopia finds a letter that is addressed "Au grand visir Orcan" (11). This letter is from the king, Amurat, who for some reason begins his letter with an explanation of why he is giving the order to have Arianisse killed: "Mon Amour vient enfin de céder à ma colère. Un homme comme moi ne doit pas écouter la pitié. Allez donc . . . sacrifier l'ingrat Arianisse . . ." (11). Amurat also warns Orcan that Musulman may try to stop him and Amurat adds that executing Arianisse is also a sure way of causing Scanderberg, Amurat's greatest enemy, a lot of pain.

Scanderberg writes a letter to Arianisse telling her that he loves her and all he asks of her is her permission to do so: " . . . m'accordez vôtre pitié puis que pour prix d'un coeur passionée & fidèle que je vous donne, je n'ose vous demander, que la liberté de vous dire que je vous adorerai éternellement" (53). The politeness and the language of Scanderberg echo that of the seventeenth-century "honnête homme". After reading Scander-berg's letter, Arianisse finally decides to respond by writing a letter herself. Her letter differs from that of Scanderberg in that it is rather vague, whereas Scanderberg's letter clearly states that he is in love with her. Arianisse begins her letter by telling Scanderberg that she is hesitant in writing it. She does indicate that she is concerned about his wellbeing: ". . . je m'intéresse pour vôtre repos . . ." (75). However, she refuses to admit that she loves him as much as he loves her; she simply ends her letter by giving Scanderberg the right to think whatever he wishes: ". . . je n'ose rien vous dire de la part de mon coeur, pensez-en ce qu'il faut, pour vous satisfaire" (75-76). Scanderberg is not able to answer Arianisse's letter, but it is at this point that he gives what could be a possible explanation of how he, like other view-point characters in la Roche-Guilhen's novels, is able to quote (or read, as the case may be) this letter while telling his story to Thopia: "Il ne me fut pas permis de répondre au Billet d'Arianisse, & je me contentai de le relire mille fois chaque jour" (76).

In *Le Grand Scanderberg*, Amisse also writes a letter to her beloved Thopia, warning him of King Castriot's anger. Castriot is angry because Thopia has seriously wounded Balsé. Castriot, who is very fond of Balsé, declares that he will have Thopia executed if Balsé dies. The very first line of Amisse's letter is a condemnation on the part of Mlle de la Roche-Guilhen, of violent acts: "Comme l'on ne doit guére espérer de repos des actions violentes . . ." (138). Amisse makes it quite clear to Thopia that she wants him to leave the country because she is afraid for his life. Amisse adds that the queen has always wanted to get Thopia out of the country, and besides, this would give the king's anger time to subside: "S'il est vrai, que j'aye du pouvoir sur vous, & que vous ayez quelque confidance en moi; laissez un peu de temps au chagrin du Roi. La Reine le souhaite, & je vous le demande. Eloignez-vous, Thopia: je crains pour vôtre vie . . ." (138).

In response to Amisse's letter, Thopia writes to Amisse, assuring her that he will obey her wishes. In this letter, Thopia is portrayed as one of the most gallant "honnêtes hommes" of seventeenth-century France. His willingness to give up his beloved Amisse in order to please her is unquestionable proof that Thopia is the perfect lover, according to the rules set forth in Mlle de Scudéry's works, for he proves himself worthy of her love by his actions. Thopia makes it clear to Amisse that his main goal is to please her; moreover, he will never stop loving her:

. . . il s'agit de vous satisfaire. Je partirai Madame, &
c'est à vôtre coeur, que je demanderai une protection, sans
la quelle je ne supporterai pas les peines de l'absence.
Adieu; si je meurs sans vous voir, ce ne sera jamais sans
vous aimer. (139)

In *Almanzaïde*, Cleonis writes to Almanzor to tell him that she
wishes to see him.   Scanderberg writes to Arianisse because
Amurat, the king, has her well guarded—protecting her from the
advances of other men.   Quite often, Aradin is allowed to see
Arianisse; so he offers to deliver Scanderberg's letter to her. Like
Cleonis, Amisse writes a letter to Thopia because of propriety;
besides, it is not safe (because of Castiot's anger) for Thopia and
Amisse to see each other. In *Zingis*, however, there is not a single
letter, and the characters seem to have greater freedom than those
in *Almanzaïde* and *Le Grand Scanderberg*. Actually, the personages in *Zingis* tend to demand freedom—this perhaps is exemplary
of la Roche-Guilhen's increasing desire to be free. When Zingis
is banished from the country (really he leaves only to please
Taxila) he does not consider writing to Taxila, for once he realizes
he can no longer live without her, he returns to the castle to take
her by force. Zingis is captured, and thrown into prison; yet he
never writes to his beloved Taxila.

There is clearly diversity in Anne de la Roche-Guilhen's
treatment of the letter as a narrative device. Although most of the
letters in the three novels under consideration are inquiries and
responses concerning matters of love, there are also letters that
relay orders to carry out an execution and to arrange a secret
rendez-vous between friends.   Nevertheless, la Roche-Guilhen
does not rely solely on the letter, for in *Almanzaïde* (1674), the
text of one letter is disclosed; the contents of five letters are
included in *Le Grand Scanderberg* (1688); and there is not a single
letter in *Zingis* (1691). In each of the three novels examined here,
however, the omniscient narrator, the view-point character, and the
dialogue are all employed as narrative devices.

First and Third-Person Narration

In the novels of Anne de la Roche-Guilhen, first-person narration is mostly used in relating the various stories, but it also appears in the dialogue. Occasionally, in the view-point character's narration, the discourse becomes very personalized. While telling his story to Aristan, Almanzor explains his emotional state of mind during his youth:

> Ie ne pensois plus rien qui ne me la confirmast, ie languissois par tout ou n'estoit pas Almanzaïde; j'étois desperé quand Abdala estoit trop longtemps à m'envoyer chez Roxane; & ie vous confesse mesm que ie murmurois quand vous m'occupiez à des leçons trop longues, dont ie ne profitois que par hasard, puisque ie ne pensois qu'à elle. (25-26)

In the above quotation, the view-point character repeats the personal pronoun "I" (*ie*) seven times in one sentence. Consequently the reader's attention is generally focused upon the narrator. This technique is also found in *Le Grand Scanderberg* and *Zingis*. While describing an emotional moment with Arianisse, Scanderberg recounts his actions: "Pour moi, j'embrassai les genoux d'Arianisse; j'y répandis des larmes; je lui jurai une fidelité inviolable, & je lui dis adieu pour la dernière fois; m'éloignant par son ordre, afin de n'être pas surpris auprés d'elle" (87). Likewise, Omir, a character in *Zingis*, finds himself at the feet of his beloved—mirrowing a penitent sinner kneeling before God—proclaiming his faithfulness and giving thanks:

> Je me jettai aux piez de la Princesse transporté d'amour . . . je lui fis un recit imaginé sur le champ d'avantures . . . Je demeurai dans le Palais parmi les filles de Thamirize, & je n'oubliai aucunes des précautions qui pouvoient assurer mon secret . . . (143)

Though first-person narration is employed rather frequently by the view-point character and in dialogues of Mlle de la Roche-Guilhen's novels, third-person narration is more prevalent. As the view-point characters relate their stories, they generally speak of what others did. Accordingly, other personages are referred to constantly with "he" or "she".

Third-person narration is especially the main device of the omnscient narrator, for he is not an active participant in the story; he reports an external point of view of who the characters are and what they are doing. In *Almanzaïde*, the omniscient narrator relies on third-person narration to describe the actions of the personages: "Cleonis demeura peu avec elle . . . mais comme elle ne pouvoit chercher Almanzor elle mesme, des qu'elle fut à son appartement, elle lui écrivit un billet qu'elle donna à un vieil Enuque pour luy porter . . ." (144). In the above quote, the omniscient narrator reveals Cleonis' concern for Almanzor's well-being once she discovers Roxane's plot against him. Since Cleonis is unable to go see Almanzor in person, she writes him a letter.

Narration in the novels of Anne de la Roche-Guilhen is sometimes problematic. One of the most visible difficulties appears in her presentation of letters. In many instances, la Roche-Guilhen offers no explanation for the view-point character's ability to quote the contents of letters. To the experienced reader, the need for clarification is quite obvious. The only hint of an explanation, as aforementioned, is found in the words of Scanderberg as he gives his reason for not answering Arianisse's letter. Scanderberg declares that although he was unable to respond to Arianisse's letter, he found joy in reading it a thousand times a day. Consequently, knowing that Scanderberg kept Arianisse's letter, the reader may conclude that the other view-point characters did the same; and while narrating their stories, they simply pulled these letters from a pocket near their hearts and revealed them to the listener.

Likewise, the narrative style of Anne de la Roche-Guilhen becomes questionable in her portrayal of the view-point characters. Occasionally, she tends to give them powers that are usually reserved for the omniscient narrator.   Often, the view-point character reports about things he has neither seen nor heard.   A good example of this problem is the aforementioned incident where Philing, a view-point character, admits that he was not in the palace when a conversation between Hildezar and Axione took place; yet Philing repeats their exact words in dialogue form—an impossible feat for a mere view-point character.

In spite of the few instances of dubious narration in her novels, Mlle de la Roche-Guilhen plies the various narrative devices (omniscient narrator, view-point character, letter, dialogue) in a skillful manner.   Although her novels contain a considerable number of stories, they are generally narrated in such a way that the reader inevitably perceives the importance of the role that these stories play.   The conflict between lovers is disclosed in each of the view-point characters' story.   There is always some counter force which comes between the lovers; frequently, this is one of the other characters.   Nonetheless, the abundance of stories in Mlle de la Roche-Guilhen only emphasizes the fated struggle between lovers.

The uniqueness of la Roche-Guilhen's narrative style is not revealed in her choices of novelistic techniques, for other seventeenth-century writers used the same novelistic conventions. Novelists like Mlle de Scudéry, Mme de Villedieu and Mme de La Fayette all make use of the omniscient narrator, the view-point character, dialogues and letter.   The uniqueness of each author, however, lies in the manner in which these devices are applied. Basically, the omniscient narrator has the same characteristics in each author, but in Mme de Villedieu's works, he makes fewer judgements of the character of the various personages.   The main function of the omniscient narrator in the novels of Mlle de Scudéry and in Mme de La Fayette is to give description; Mlle de la Roche-Guilhen's works are practically devoid of description.

The role of the view-point character is essentially the same in each author.   The view-point character, an active participant in the story, is the one who tells the numerous stories found in the novels of these authors.   The role of the view-point character differs only in the amount of work required of him. In the works of Mlle de Scudéry, who mainly wrote the ten-volume type novel, the viewpoint character is overworked, whereas in la Roche-Guilhen's works he is called upon less often and even less frequently in Mme de La Fayette.

The dialogue abounds in the works of Mlle de Scudéry. In fact, the dialogue is the main form of narration in her novels as well as in those of Mme de La Fayette. Their personages are constantly engaged in conversation. These numerous dialogues produce a dramatic effect, especially in Mme de La Fayette. Since conversations are encountered throughout these novels, whether consciously or subconsciously, the reader is apt to get the impression that he is watching actors perform on stage or maybe in a film. In the dialogue in Mlle de Scudéry's works, various rules of love, courtship and marriage are discussed. In Mme de La Fayette's novels, though love is the topic of discussion, the conversations are individualistic rather than universal. Although Mme de La Fayette's characters are constantly preoccupied with love, they discuss it only in an effort to find a solution to their personal problems concerning love. This also holds true in the dialogue of Mlle de la Roche-Guilhen's characters. They do not discuss love on a philosophical or universal level; it is the personal effects of love in their lives that dominate the conversations of la Roche-Guilhen's characters.

The letter is yet another narrative device that was especially popular during the second half of the seventeenth-century. All of the above-mentioned authors took advantage of this novelistic convention. Nevertheless, each author's originality is revealed in the contents of these letters. In each case, though the letter is generally used as a complication of the plot, these letters are in some way connected to love. For example, in Mlle de la Roche-Guilhen's *Le Grand Scanderberg*, the king writes a letter to Orcan giving the order to have Arianisse executed. He also explains that he is requesting this execution because his passion for Arianisse has kindled his anger. There are two letters from the Duc de Guise to Mme de Sauve in Mme de Villedieu's *Les Desordres de l'amour.* In the first, the Duc de Guise proclaims his faithfulness, but in the second letter he accuses Mme de Sauve of having deceived him. In Mlle de Scudéry's *Clélie*, Brutus writes a letter to Lucrèce; it is this letter to Lucrèce, which is found by Lucrèce's father, that causes Brutus to lose his beloved to another. In Mme de La Fayette's *La Princesse de Clèves*, a letter is written to the vidame de Chartres—everyone, including Mme de Clèves, thought it was to M. de Nemours—accusing him of being unfaithful. Thus, there is indeed variety in the contents of these letters.

Consequently, the myth that Anne de la Roche-Guilhen's novels are nothing more than an imitation of Mlle de Scudéry is certainly unfounded, for la Roche-Guilhen's originality is not only visible in her treatment of plot and characterization, but also in her narrative style.

Conclusion

Anne de la Roche-Guilhen is indeed a worthy and prolific seventeenth-century novelist who has been unjustly neglected by modern critics. Although Alexandre Calame has done much to clarify the many proposed dates of la Roche-Guilhen's birth, there are still unsolved mysteries about her life and undiscovered characteristics of her works. Before the publication of Calame's study, *Anne de la Roche-Guilhen, romancière huguenote 1644-1707*, several inaccurate dates of la Roche-Guilhen's birth were proposed: 1640, 1653, 1663. Calame found records in the Protestant church of Quevilly, proving that Mlle de la Roche-Guilhen was baptized in 1644. This discovery completely destroyed the theory that she was born in 1653 or in 1663.

La Roche-Guilhen is mentioned in René Godenne's *Histoire de la nouvelle française aux XVII et XVIII siècles* as well as in English Showalter, Junior's *The Evolution of the French Novel 1641-1782*, but her novels are not analyzed in either of these works of criticism; her name is simply listed among others who wrote certain types of novels (heroic, gallant, etc.). Her works are still neglected by modern critics.

Although Mlle de la Roche-Guilhen was born into a noble Huguenot family, she had very little opportunity to enjoy life, for her family suffered persecution, like other Huguenots, because of its religious beliefs; and, in her latter years, she seemingly had to take care of her sickly sisters. Thus when Anne de la Roche-Guilhen and two of her four sisters fled to England to find refuge, it appears that her writing became a necessity for the financial support of her sisters and herself. Being isolated from her fellow

French novelists, la Roche-Guilhen undoubtedly had to write without the collaboration of the learned men who offered their assistance to other female novelists of seventeenth-century France. Mme de La Fayette was assisted by Segrais, Ménage, Huet and La Rochefoucauld while Mlle de Scudéry was aided by her brother George. Even without the assistance of a knowledgeable male collaborator, la Roche-Guilhen was able to write novels that pleased the seventeenth-century reader, for she wrote over twenty-five works, nearly all of which appeared in several editions; moreover, some were translated into English.

Anne de la Roche-Guilhen's life is quite often reflected in her works. Her novels, however, are not autobiographical, for in most cases her characters are given attributes that are diametrically opposed to her own. Whereas la Roche-Guilhen had close family ties, her heroes and heroines do not. Oftentimes her characters do not know who their parents are, and those who know their parents are separated from them quite early in life. Frequently, during his youth, la Roche-Guilhen's hero leaves home to make a name for himself. Sometimes the hero is given to some powerful king as a slave. The portrayal of the heroine tends to follow the same pattern. If she is afforded the privilege of being reared with parental guidance, it is the father who provides it. Neither prince nor princess experiences the love of a mother. Similarly, Anne de la Roche-Guilhen, a spinster, spent eighteen years with her father after the death of her mother. It is quite possible that she, like her heroines, suffered under the guidance of a strict father.

Anne de la Roche-Guilhen undoubtedly never experienced the courtly love about which she wrote; at least it seems that she never married. Instead, being a devoted family member, she spent the latter years of her life taking care of her sisters. In contrast, her heroines are great princesses like those found in fairy tales. They are always in captivity; a handsome prince inevitably comes to their rescue; they invariably fall in love; finally they get married and live happily ever after. Although it appears that Mlle de la Roche-Guilhen realized her fantasies through her novels, she actually wrote works that are somewhat similar to those of other writers of her time. Other novelists, especially Mlle de Scudéry and Madame de La Fayette, also wrote about great princes and princesses. Though there are similarities in characterization, there are many unique elements in the works of these authors. Basically, Mlle de Scudéry's characters depict real people of her day; those of Mme de La Fayette, who seem to be mere creations of the author, are subjected to psychological analysis; the characters of Anne de la Roche-Guilhen, who are also created by the author, exemplify the universal struggle of mankind.

Mlle de la Roche-Guilhen's treatment of love is quite unique, for her characters are possessed by a passion that differs from that in other seventeenth-century novelists. La Roche-Guilhen's hero always meets some beautiful princess with whom he immediately falls in love. The hero in la Roche-Guilhen's works never experiences the horrid feeling of being in love with a princess who does not love him. Neither the prince nor the princess escapes Cupid's mighty arrow. Although the hero and the heroine love each other, there are many obstacles. Quite often the princess is a captive and the prince has to fight to set her free. Occasionally it is the evil queen who stands between these lovers. Nonetheless, the hero and heroine must struggle to overcome many obstacles. Basically, Mlle de Scudéry's characters tend to be in control of their passions and they always seem to act in an honourable manner. Though Mlle de Scudéry's heroes, Cyrus for example, have to chase after their beloved who is kidnapped constantly, they are not driven to the point of acting imprudently. The heroes of Mlle de la Roche-Guilhen, however, are so overwhelmed by passion that they often appear irrational. For example, when Zingis, one of la Roche-Guilhen's heroes, learns that plans are being made to announce the wedding of his beloved Taxila and the cowardly Timur, he attacks and nearly kills Timur. Adhering to the wishes of Taxila, Zingis flees to safety. Realizing he can no longer live without Taxila, Zingis returns to kidnap her; but he becomes impatient at the gate of the palace and begins to yell for someone to open it. As a result of his irrational behavior, Zingis is captured, put in chains, thrown into prison and sentenced to die.

By contrast, Madeleine de Scudéry's characters are frequently engaged in long philosophical discussions about love and actually are denied the opportunity to openly declare their love for one another. Mandane and Cyrus are in love for many years, yet they refrain from showing any sign to each other.

Instead of engaging in long philosophical discussions, la Roche-Guilhen's characters usually talk about the difficulty they are experiencing. These conversations, like those in the works of Mlle de Scudéry, Mme de La Fayette and others, are always in some way connected with love. Nevertheless, while Madeleine de Scudéry's characters discuss the rules of love, the personages of Anne de la Roche-Guilhen and those of Mme de La Fayette converse in an effort to find a solution to their personal problems.

The dialogue is one of the main forms of narration in the novels of Mlle de Scudéry, but it is used less often in those of Mlle de la Roche-Guilhen. Mlle de la Roche-Guilhen's novels are mainly composed of interrelated tales narrated by one character to another. The works of Mme de La Fayette, like those of Mlle de Scudéry, however, abound with conversations. Nevertheless, there is a noticeable difference between the conversations in the novels of Mme de La Fayette and those of Mlle de Scudéry. Similar to those in the works of la Roche-Guilhen, Mme de La Fayette's characters generally converse about their personal problems pertaining to love. The novels of la Roche-Guilhen and Mme de La Fayette also contain a tragic element not found in the works of Mlle de Scudéry.

As the action unfolds—actually from the very beginning of the novel, once the scene has been set—the reader is immediately made aware of the tragic state of the personages of Anne de la Roche-Guilhen. La Roche-Guilhen's hero is most often confronted by an insurmountable obstacle in his search for happiness with the beautiful princess who has captured his heart. Throughout la Roche-Guilhen's novels, the hero, and oftentimes the heroine, is repeatedly beset by various obstacles, yet his struggle to overcome them does not end until he has gained his beloved's hand in marriage.

The characters in Mme de La Fayette's *La Princesse de Clèves* are tragic, but they do not possess the same stamina as the personages of Anne de la Roche-Guilhen. Mme de la Fayette's characters tend to surrender before the battle is won. M. de Clèves hopes to be loved (not just esteemed) by his wife, but Mme de Clèves is torn between her passion for M. de Nemours and her duty to her husband, and M. de Nemours desires to be loved by Mme de Clèves. When M. de Clèves has convinced himself that his wife is deeply in love with M. de Nemours and will never love him, he dies—lacking the ability and willingness to fight for her. When Madame de Clèves is confronted with the reality of death, she finally realizes that her honor (loyalty to her husband) is very important to her; so she finds refuge from Nemours in a convent—denying herself the possiblity of finding happiness with M. de Nemours. When M. de Nemours hears, from Mme de Clèves herself, that his beloved has chosen seclusion in a convent, he readily—at least without making any further attempts to persuade her to chose him—accepts her decision.

Mlle de la Roche-Guilhen, Mlle de Scudéry and Mme de La Fayette not only differ in their treatment of love and the contents of their characters' conversations, but their characters exemplify different phases of love. The personages of both Mlle de Scudèry and Mlle de la Roche-Guilhen are in the courtship stage, but those of Mlle de Scudéry, in many instances, never get close enough to consider marriage. In fact, Mlle de Scudéry frequently protrays marriage as an undesirable institution—especially for women. Although Mlle de la Roche-Guilhen's heroes and heroines are also portrayed in the stage of courtship, they inevitably get married. Mme de La Fayette's *La Princesse de Cléves* practically begins with the marriage of M. de Clèves to Mlle de Chartres, and the remainder of the novel is devoted to un unfavorable portrayal of marriage—marriage leads to despair.

Another unique factor in Anne de la Roche-Guihen's novels is the manner in which her characters are held in captivity, prisoners, unable to move about freely. Zingis is even physically thrown into prison. Although Scanderberg and Almanzor are not imprisoned physically, they are held captive by their passion. Once his beloved Arianisse has been taken by the evil king, Scanderberg is so heartbroken that he plunges into an extremely melancholic state. Because of his despression, he wants to go nowhere and to do nothing. Scanderberg does not remain in this state forever; finally he decides to take Arianisse from her captor by force. Almanzor is as heartbroken as Scanderberg because his beloved Almanzaïde has been promised to another. After killing Timur, Almanzaïde's fiancé, Almanzor, is free to marry her himself.

In contrast, the characters in the novels of Mlle de Scudéry and Mme de La Fayette have greater freedom to move about. They are not thrown into prison and they do not become as melancholic as the characters of Mlle de la Roche-Guilhen. Moreover the personas of Scudéry and La Fayette seem to take sadistic pleasure in their romantic misfortunes. Accordingly, although being in each other's presence is disquieting, M. de Nemours and Mme de Clèves continously search for occasions to be together. The characters of both Mlle de Scudéry and Mme de La Fayette possess a freedom that is reminiscent of that of Honoré d'Urfé's shepherds and shepherdesses in the peaceful forest of Forez. No one works or takes part in military battles; everyone spends each day doing whatever he finds pleasureable. Usually these characters meet and participate in long discussions about love. They are clearly not prisoners.

The general framework of the novels of these seventeenth-century French women writers (Scudéry, la Roche-Guilhen and La Fayette) is basically the same—the prince who is in love with the princess struggles to prove himself worthy of her love. Mlle de Scudéry who wrote the lenghty ten-volume type novel is known for long philosophical discussions about love and the famous "Carte de Tendre." Mme de La Fayette is recognized for having developed the psychological novel. One of Anne de la Roche-Guilhen's contribution to the development of the French novel is the perfecting of the art of storytelling—a device that had already been used by Rabelais—as a narrative device. Her special treatment of love, tragedy and plot bears a significant uniqueness when compared to that of other seventeenth-century novelists.

Perhaps Anne de la Roche-Guilhen's greatest contribution to the development of the French novel is the skillfull manner in which she applies the art of storytelling as a narrative device, for her novels are composed almost entirely of stories narrated by one character to another. Each of the three novels that have been analyzed in this study illustrates this artful technique. Shortly after the beginning of each novel (*Almanzaïde*, *Scanderberg* and *Zingis*), the hero or some other personage sets out to tell his story. From this point onward, there is a succession of stories. In essence, everything the reader learns about the characters is revealed in one of these stories. There is very little narration linking one story to the next. When a character finishes his story, the omniscient narrator steps in only long enough to prepare the reader for the next story. With Mlle de la Roche-Guilhen's skillfull use of storytelling, the reader is exposed to several points of view. More importantly, when the hero is allowed to tell his own story, the violent passion and anguish of the storyteller is revealed—this would not be the case if the story were told by another character or by the omniscient narrator. Ordinarily one would think that so many stories would bore the reader, but la Roche-Guilhen has so ingeniously mastered this art that one would likely forget that he is reading a story which is being told by a certain character had it not been for the constant reminders—the storyteller often refers to his character-listener by name.

Anne de la Roche-Guilhen's unique treatment of plot is another distinguishing feature of her works. Contrary to other seventeenth-century novelists who wrote works with fairy-tale-like themes throughout and tragic endings, la Roche-Guilhen produced novels that are tragic throughout with fairy-tale-like endings. La Roche-Guilhen portrays the struggle of her characters as they attempt to overcome the many obstacles that come between them and their happiness. When the struggle has ended and the personage has fought to the bitter end, la Roche-Guilhen's characters are always rewarded with eternal bliss.

In *Almanzaïde*, *Scanderberg* and *Zingis*, la Roche-Guilhen's characters are held prisoners in a sort of living hell. They fall in love and they are tormented by the very presence of the one they love. As the plot unfolds, the personages' suffering increases to the point that it becomes unbearable. It is only after arriving at this point that la Roche-Guilhen's characters are set free. Oftentimes, having taken all that he can bear, the hero wins his freedom with the sword. Occasionally, it is the *deus ex machina* who, at a very crucial moment, comes to the hero's rescue. Considering Anne de la Roche-Guilen's unique contributions to the development of the novel, it is quite clear that the myth that she is a mere imitator of Madeleine de Scudéry is unfounded. In fact, la Roche-Guilhen is a noteworthy pioneer of her day and a precursor of writers of the eighteenth-century novel in her use of first-person narrative.

Notes

INTRODUCTION

1. The spelling of the author's name is in accordance with the findings of Alexandre Calame: *Anne de la Roche-Guilhen: romancière huguenote* (9). Nearly all other literary sources refer to her as la Roche-Guilhem.

2. See bibliography for a list of these works.

3. The spelling in the quotations of Anne de la Roche-Guilhen's works has not been modernized. However, the typography of seventeenth-century France has been altered somewhat for the sake of neatness.

CHAPTER TWO

1. Since Anne de la Roche-Guilhen was a Huguenot of seventeenth-century France, she undoubtedly experienced inner conflict. Whereas her characters' inner conflict is caused by their inability to obtain freedom to love, hers was brought about by the lack of freedom to worship God without interference from those who had different religious beliefs.

Works by Anne de la Roche-Guilhen[1]

La Roche-Guilhen, Anne de. *Almanzaide*. Paris: Barbin, 1674.

———. *Arioviste*. Paris: Barbin, 1674-1675.

———. *Asterie ou Tamerlam*. Paris: Barbin, 1675.

———. *Journal amoureux d'Espagne*. Editions hollondaises, 1675.

———. "Rare en tout." Londres: n.p., 1677.

———. *Le Comte d'Essex*. Paris: Barbin, 1678.

———. *Histoires des guerres civiles de Grenade*. Paris: Barbin, 1683.

———. *Zamire*. La Haye: Troyel, 1687.

———. *Le Grand Scanderberg*. Amsterdam: Sabouret, 1688.

———. *Intrigues amoureuses des quelque anciens Grecs*. La Haye: Van Bulderen, 1690.

———. *Nouvelles historiques*. La Haye: Van Bulderen, 1691.

———. *Zingis*. La Haye: Van Bulderen, 1691.

———. *Le Duc de Guise*. La Haye: Alberts, 1693.

———. *Histoire chronologique d'Espagne*. Rotterdam: Acher, 1694.

———. *Histoire des amours du Duc d'Arione*. La Haye: Troyel, 1694.

———. *L'Innocente justifiée, histoires de Grenade*. La Haye: Troyel, 1694.

---

[1]For bibliographical information of the subsequent editions and translations, see Alexandre Calame, *Anne de la Roche-Guilhen, romancière huhuenote 1644-1707* (Genève: Droz, 1972) 91-94.

————. *Les amours de Néron*. La Haye: Troyel, 1695.

————. *Histoires des favorites*. Amsterdam: Marret, 1697.

————. *L'Amitié singulière*. Amsterdam: Troyel, 1700.

————. *La Nouvelle talestris*. Amsterdam: Marret, 1700.

————. *Sapho*. La Haye: de Voys, 1706.

————. *Jacqueline de Bavière*. Amsterdam: Marret, 1707.

————. *Dernières oeuvres*. Amsterdam: Marret, 1708.

————. *La Foire de Beaucaire*. Amsterdam: Marret, 1708.

————. *Oeuvres diverses*. Amsterdam: Bernard, 1711.

Works Cited

Adam, Antoine. *Histoire de la littérature française au XVIIe siècle*. 5 vols. Paris: Editions Domat, 1957.

Boulton, Majorie. *The Anatomy of the Novel*. London: Routledge & Kegan Paul, 1975.

Calame, Alexandre. *Anne de la Roche-Guilhen, romancière huguenote 1644-1707*. Genéve: Droz, 1972.

Cioranescu, Alexandre. *Bibliographie de la littérature française du dix-septiéme siècle*. 3 vols. Paris: Editions du Centre National de la Recherche Scientifique, 1955-66.

Dejean, Joan. *Libertine Strategies: Freedom and the Novel Seventeenth-Century France*. Columbus: Ohio State University Press, 1981.

———. *Tender Geographies: Women and the Origins of the Novel in France*. New York: Columbia University Press, 1991.

Delcro, A. *Dictionnaire universel et litteraire des romans*. 3 vols. N.p.: n.p., n.d.

Forster, E. M. *Aspects of the Novel*. New York: Frederick Ungar Publishing Co., 1964.

Godenne, René. *Histoire de la nouvelle française aux XVIIe et XVIIIe siècles*. Genève: Droz, 1970.

Green, Frederick C. *French Novelists, Manners and Ideas: From the Renaissance to the Revolution*. New York: Frederick Ungar, 1964.

Grente, Cardinal George. *Dictionnaire des lettres françaises*. Paris: Fayard, 1954.

Hoefer, Ferdinand. *Nouvelle biographie générale*. 85 vols. Paris: Firmin Didot Frères, 1862.

The Holy Bible. King James Version.

Kastner, L. E., Henry Gibson Atkins. *A Short History of French Literature: From the Origin to the Present Day.* Port Washington, New York: Kennikat Press, 1970.

Lever, Maurice. *Le roman français au XVIIe siècle.* Paris: Presses Universitaires, 1981.

Macauley, Robie, George Lanning. *Technique in Fiction.* New York: Harper & Row, 1964.

Michaud, Louis-Gabriel. *Biographie universelle ancienne et moderne.* 85 vols. Paris: Chez Michaud Frères, 1811-62.

Niderst, Alain. *La Princesse de Clèves de Madame de Lafayette.* Paris: Librairie A. G. Nizet, 1977.

Pitou, Spire. "A Forgotten Play: La Roche-Guilhen's 'Rare en tout' (1677)." *Modern Language Notes* 72 (1957): 357-60.

Porte, l'abbé de la. *Histoire des femmes françaises.* 3 vols. Paris: n.p., 1769.

Roche-Guilhen, Anne de la. *Almanzaide, Nvvelle* [sic]. Paris: Barbin, 1674.

———. *Le Grand Scanderberg, Mouvelle.* Amsterdam: Chez Pierre Savouret, 1688.

———. *Zingis, Histoire tartare.* La Haye: Chez Jean Swart, 1711.

Showalter, English, Jr. *The Evolution of the French Novel 1641-1782.* Princeton University Press, 1972.

Selected Bibliography

Adam, Antoine. *Grandeur and Illusion, French Literature and Society 1600-1715*. Trans. Herbert Tint. Great Britain: George Weidenfeld and Nicolson Ltd., 1972.

————. *Romanciers du XVIIe siècle: Sorel - Scarron - Furetière - Madame de la Fayette*. Paris: Editions Gallimard, 1958.

Albouy, Pierre. *Mythes et mythologies dans la littérature française*. Paris: Librairie Armand Colin, 1969.

Aronson, Nicole. *Mademoiselle de Scudéry*. Boston: Twayne Publishers, 1978.

————. *Mademoiselle de Scudéry, ou, Le Voyage au pays de Tendre*. Fayard, 1986.

Arnott, Peter D. *The Ancient Greek and Roman Theatre*. New York: Random House, 1971.

————. *An Introduction to the Greek Theatre*. Bloomington: Indiana University Press, 1959.

Beasley, Faith E. *Revising Memory: Women's Fiction and Memoirs in Seventeenth-Century France*. New Brunswick: Rutgers University Press, 1990.

Benjamin, Jessica. *The Bonds of Love: Psychoanalysis, Feminism, and the Problem of Domination*. New York: Pantheon, 1988.

Bersani, Leo. *A Future for Astyanax: Character and Desire in Literature*. Boston: Little Brown, 1976.

Bertaud, Madeleine. *Le XVIIe siècle: littérature française*. Nancy: Presses universitaires de Nancy, 1990.

Bishop, Lloyd. *In Search of Style: Essays in French Literary Stylistics*. Charlottesville: University Press of Virginia, 1982.

Boixareu, Mercédès. *Fonction de la narration du dialogue dans 'La Princesse de Clèves.'* Archives de Lettres Modernes, vol. 239: Lettres Modernes, 1989.

Boone, Joseph Allen. *Tradition Counter Tradition: Love and the Form of Fiction.* Chicago: University of Chicago Press, 1989.

Booth, Wayne. *The Rhetoric of Fiction.* Chicago: University of Chicago Press, 1961.

————. "Distance and Point of View." *Essays in Criticism* 11 (1961): 60-79.

Bourneuf, Roland and Real Ouellet. *L'Univers du roman.* Paris: Presses Universitaires de France, 1981.

Bremond, Claude. "The Logic of Narrative Possibilities." *New Literary History* 11 (1980): 387-411.

————. *La Logique du récit.* Paris: Seuil, 1973.

Brewer, Maria Minich. "'A Loosening of Tongues': From Narrative Economy to Women's Writing." *MLN* 99 (1984): 1141-61.

Brody, Jules. "*La Princesse de Clèves* and the Myth of Courtly Love." *University of Toronto Quarterly* 38 (1969): 105-35.

Brooks, Peter. *The Novel of Wordliness.* Princeton, N.J.: Princeton University Press, 1969.

————. *Reading for the Plot: Design and intention in Narrative.* New York: Knopf, 1984.

Butrick, May Wendelene. "The Concept of Love in the Maxims of La Rochefoucauld." Ph.D. diss., State University of Iowa, 1959.

Charnes, Jean-Antoine, Abbé de. *Conversations sur la critique de la Princesse de Clèves.* Edited by François Weil et al. Tours: Université de Tours, 1973.

Chatman, Seymour. *Story and Discourse: Narrative Structure in Fiction.* Ithaca: Cornell University Press, 1978.

Cholakian, Patricia Francis. *The Early French Nouvella.* Albany: State University of New York, 1972.

Collins, R. G. *The Novel and Its Changing Form.* Winnipeg, Canada: University of Manitoba Press, 1972.

Coulet, Henri. *Le Roman jusqu'à la révolution.* 2 vols. Paris:

A. Colin, 1967.

Cousin, Victor. *La Société française au XVIIe siècle d'après 'Le Grand Cyrus' de Mademoiselle de Scudéry*. 2 vols. Didier, 1858.

Cuénin, Micheline. *Roman et Société sous Louis XIV: Mme de Villedieu*. 2 vols. Paris: Champion, 1979.

Dallas, Dorothy F. *Le Roman français de 1669 à 1680*. Paris: J. Gamber, 1932.

Dédéyan, Charles. *Madame de Lafayette*. Paris: Société d'édition d'enseignement supérieur, 1956.

DeJean, Joan. "La Lettre amoureuse revue et cirrigée: Un texte oublié de M. de Scudéry." *Revue d'histoire littéraire de la France* (January-February 1988), pp. 17-22.

———, ed. *Women's Writings in Seventeenth-Century France*. Special issue, *Esprit Créateur* 23, no. 2 (1983).

———, and Nancy K. Miller, eds. *The Politics of Tradition: Placing Women in French Literature*. Special issue, *Yale French Studies* 75 (1988).

Delhez-Sarlet, Claudette. "Les Jaloux et la jalousie dans l'oeuvre romanesque de Mme de la Fayette." *Revue des sciences humaines* 29 (1964): 279-309.

———. "Style indirect libre et 'point de vue' dans *La Princesse de Clèves*." *Cahiers d'analyse textuelle* 6 (1964): 70-80.

Deloffre, Frederic. *La Nouvelle en France à l'âge classique*. Paris: Librairie Marcel Didier, 1967.

Desjardins, Marie-Catherine Hortense (Known as Mme de Villedieu). *Les Desordres de l'amour*. Genève: Droz, 1970.

Dezon-Jones, Elyane. *Les écritures féminines*. Paris: éditions magnard, 1983.

Docherty, Thomas. *Reading (Absent) Character: Towards a theory of Characterization in Fiction*. Oxford: Clarendon, 1983.

Duchêne, Roger. *Mme de La Fayette: la romancière aux cent bras*. Librairie Arthème Fayard, 1988.

Dulong, Claude. *L'Amour au XVIIe siècle*. Paris: Hachette,

1969.

DuPlessis, Rachel Blau. *Writing beyond the Ending: Narrative Stategies of Twentieth-Century Women Writers.* Bloomington: Indiana University Press, 1985.

Edwards, Lee R. *Psyche As Hero: Female Heroism and Fictional Form.* Middletown, Connecticut: Wesleyan University Press, 1984.

Fagniez, Gustave. *La Femme et la société française dans la première moitié du XVIIe siècle.* Paris: J. Gamber, 1929.

Felman, Shoshana. "Beyond Oedipus: The Specimen Story of Psychoanalysis." *Lacan and Narration: The Psychoanalytic Difference in Narrative Theory.* ed., Robert Con Davis. Baltimore: Johns Hopkins University Press, 1983.

Flannigan, Arthur. *Mme de Villedieu's 'Les Desordres de l'amour', History, Literature, and the Nouvelle historique.* Washington, D. C.: University Press of America, Inc., 1982.

————. "Mme de Villedieu's *'Les Desordres de l'amour'*: The Feminization of History." *Esprit Créateur* 23, no. 2 (1983): 94-106.

Fowler, Roger, ed. *Style and Structure in Literature: Essays in the New Stylistics.* Ithaca: Cornell University Press, 1975.

François, Carlo. *Précieuses et autres indociles: aspects du féminisme dans la littérature française du XVIIᵉ siècle.* Birmingham: Summa Publications, Inc., 1987.

Friedman, Norman. "Point of View in Fiction: The Development of a Critical Concept." *PMLA* 70:1160-84.

Frohock, W. M. *Style and Temper: Studies in French Fiction.* Cambridge: Harvard University Press, 1967.

Genette, Gérard. *Figures of Literary Discourse.* Trans. Alan Sheridan. Intro. Marie-Rose Logan. New York: Columbia University Press, 1982.

————. *Nouveau Discours du récit.* Paris: Seuil, 1983.

Goldin, Jeanne. "Maximes et fonctionnement narratif dans *La Princesse de Clèves*." *Papers on French Seventeenth-Century Literature* 10 (1978): 155-76.

Goldman, Lucien. *Le Dieu caché: Etude sur la vision tragique dans les Pensées de Pascal et dans le théâtre de Racine.* France: Editions Gallimard, 1959.

Goldsmith, Elizabeth. *Exclusive Conversations: The Art of Interaction in Seventeenth-Century France.* Philadelphia: University of Pennsylvania Press, 1988.

Grabo, Carl H. *The Technique of the Novel.* New York: Gordian Press, Inc., 1954.

Greimas, A.-J. "Eléments d'une grammaire narrative." *L'Homme* 9:3 (1963): 71-92.

Guetti, Barbara Jones. "'Travesty' and 'Usurpation' in Mme de Lafayette's Historical Fiction." *Yale French Studies* 69 (1985): 211-221.

Guggenheim, Michel. *Women in French Literature.* Saratoga: ANMA Libri & Co., 1988

Haag, E. *La France protestante. 1846-59.* Genéve: Slatkine Reprints, 1966.

Haig, Sterling. *Madame de Lafayette.* New York: Twayne, 1970.

Halperin, John, ed. *The theory of the Novel: New Essays.* New York: Oxford University Press, 1974.

Hamilton, Clayton. *The Art of Fiction.* Intro. Brander Matthews. New York: Doubleday, Doran & Company, Inc., 1939.

Hardy, Barbara. *Tellers and Listeners: The Narrative Imagination.* University of London: The Athlone Press, 1975.

Harris, William Foster. *The Basic Formulas of Fiction.* Norman: University of Oklahoma Press, 1944.

Haureau, B. *Histoire littéraire du Maine.* Paris: Julien, Lanier, 1852.

Henry, Patrick. *An Inimitable Example: The Case for the Princesse de Clèves.* Washington, D. C.: The Catholic University of America Press, 1992.

Hepp, Noémi. "La Notion d'Héroïne." *Onze Etudes sur l'image de la femme dans la littérature française du XVIIᵉ siècle.* Edited by Wolfgang Leiner. Tubingen: Gunter Narr Verlag, 1978.

Hirsch, Marianne. "Incorporation and Repetition in *La Princesse de Clèves.*" *Yale French Studies* 62 (1981): 67-87.

Horowitz, Louise K. *Love and Language: A Study of the Classical French Moralist Writers.* Columbus: Ohio State University Press, 1977.

Houston, John Porter. *Fictional Technique in France: 1802-1927.* Baton Rouge: Louisiana State University Press, 1972.

Jasinski, René. *Histoire de la littérature française.* Paris: A.G. Nizet, 1965.

Joran, Théodore. "La Princesse de Clèves ou une pseudo-héroïne de la piété conjugale." *Revue bleue* (1925): 510-15.

Kany, Charles. *The Beginnings of the Epistolary Novel in France, Italy, and Spain.* University of California Publications in Modern Philology (1937), 21:1-158.

Koppisch, Michael S. "The Dynamics of Jealousy in the Works of Madame de Lafayette." *Modern Language Notes* 94 (1979): 757-73.

Kreiter, Janine Anseaume. *Le problème du paraître dans l'oeuvre de Mme de Lafayette.* Paris: A. G. Nizet, 1977.

Kuizenga, Donna. *Narrative Strategies in 'La Princesse de Clèves'.* Lexington, Ky.: French Forum, 1976.

Kumar, Shiv, and Keith Mckean, eds. *Critical Approaches to Fiction.* New York: McGraw-Hill, 1965.

Kusch, Manfred. "Narrative Technique and Cognitive Modes in *La Princesse de Clèves.*" *Symposium* 30 (1976): 308-24.

Lathrop, Henry Burrowes. *The Art of the Novelist.* New York: Dodd, Mead and Company, 1919.

Laurent, Jacques. *Roman du roman.* Paris: Édition Gallimard, 1977.

Le Breton, André Victor. *Le Roman au XVIIe siècle.* Paris: Hachette, 1927.

Lenglet Dufresnoy, Abbé Nicolas. *De l'usage des romans.* Amsterdam: De Poilras, 1734

Lever, Maurice. *La Fiction narrative en prose au XVIIe siècle.* Paris: Presses universitaires de France, 1981.

Lyons, John D. "Narrative, Interpretation and Paradox: *La Princesse de Clèves.*" *Romanic Review* 72 (1981): 383-400.

Mackie, J. L. *The Cement of the Universe: A Study of Causation.* Oxford: Clarendon Press, 1974.

Magendie , Maurice. *Le Roman français au XVIIe siècle de l'Astrée au Grand Cyrus.* Paris: Librairie E. Droz, 1932.

Magny, Claude-Edmonde. *Histoire du roman français.* Paris: Editions du Seuil, 1948.

Martin, Wallace. *Recent Theories of Narrative.* Ithaca: Cornell University Press, 1986.

McDougall, Dorothey. *Madeleine de Scudéry, Her Romantic Life and Death.* New York: Benjamin Blom, Inc., 1972.

Mercier, Michel. *Le Roman féminin.* Paris: Presses Universitaires de France, 1976.

Mesnard, Jean. *Précis de littérature française du XVIIe siècle.* Paris: Presses Universitaires de France, 1990.

Miller, D. A. *Narrative and Its Discontents.* Princeton: Princeton University Press, 1981.

Miller, Nancy K. "Emphasis Added: Plots and Plausibilities in Women's Fiction." *PMLA* 96 (1981): 36-48.

———. *The Heroine's Text.* New York: Columbia University Press, 1980.

———. "Tender Economies: Mme de Villedieu and the Cost of Indifference." *PMLA* 96, no. 2 (1983): 80-93.

Mongrédien, Georges. *Le XVIIe Siècle galant: libertins et amoureuses.* Paris: Perrin et Cie, 1929.

Monroe, N. Elizabeth. *The Novel and Society: A Critical Study of the Modern Novel.* Chapel Hill: University of North Carolina Press, 1941.

Mornet, Daniel. *Histoire de la littérature française classique, 1660-1700.* Paris: Armand Colin, 1942.

Morrissette, Bruce A. *The Life and Works of Marie-Catherine Desjardins (Mme de Villedieu) 1632-1683.* St. Louis: Washington University Press, 1947.

Mortimer, Armine Kotin. "Narrative Closure and the Paradigm of Self-Knowledge in *La Princesse de Clèves.*" *Style* 17 (1983): 181-95.

Moye, Richard H. "Silent Victory: Narrative, Appropriation, and

Autonomy in *La Princesse de Clèves*." *Modern Language Notes* 104 (1989): 845-60.

Nelson, William. *Fact or Fiction: The Dilemma of the Renaissance Storyteller*. Cambridge: Havard University Press, 1973.

Niderst, Alain. *'La Princesse de Clèves' de Madame de Lafayette*. Paris: Librairie A. G. Nizet, 1977.

O'Conner, William Van, ed. *Forms of Modern Fiction*. Minneapolis: University of Minnesota Press, 1948.

O'Flaherty, Kathleen. *The Novel in France: 1945-1965, A General Survey*. Cork, Ireland: Cork University Press, 1973.

Pariset, F. G. "Héroïsme et création artistique." In *Héroïsme et création littéraire sous les règnes d'Henri IV et de Louis XIII*. Klincksieck, 1974.

Pelous, Jean-Michel. *Amour précieux, amour galant (1654-1675)*. Paris: Klincksieck, 1980.

Picard, Raymond. *Two Centuries of French Literature*. Trans. John Cairncross. New York: McGraw-Hill Book Company, 1970.

Pingaud, Bernard. *Mme de Lafayette par elle-même*. Paris: Editions du Seuil, 1959.

Price, Martin. *Forms of Life: Character and Moral Imagination in the Novel*. New Haven: Yale University Press, 1983.

Prince, G. *Narratology: The Form and Function of Narrative*. The Hague: Mouton, 1982.

Ratner, Moses. *Theory and Criticism of the Novel in France from l'Astrée to 1750*. Ann Arbor: University Microfilms, 1970.

Raynal, Marie A. *La Nouvelle française de Segrais à Mme de La Fayette*. Paris: Picart, 1927.

———. *Le Talent de Mme de La Fayette*. Paris: Picart, 1927.

Reinhold, Meyer. *Classical Drama: Greek and Roman*. Woodbury, New York: Barron's Educational Series Inc., 1959.

Respaut, Michèle. "Un Texte qui se dérobe: Narrateur, lecteur et personnage dans *La Princesse de Clèves*." *L'Esprit créateur* 19 (1979): 64-73.

Reynier, Gustave. *Le Roman réaliste au XVIIe siècle*. Paris:

Hachette, 1914.

———. *Le Roman sentimental avant 'l'Astrée'*. Paris: Armand Colin, 1908.

Ricardou, Jean. *Nouveaux problèmes du roman*. Paris: Editions du Seuil, 1978.

Richetti, John. *Popular Fiction Before Richardson: Narrative Patterns 1700-1739*. Oxford: Clarendon Press, 1969.

Ricoeur, Paul. *Time and Narrative*, vol. 1. Chicago: University of Chicago, 1983.

Rimmon-Kenan, Shlomith. *Narrative Fiction: Contemporary Poetics*. New York: Methuen, 1983.

Rochefoucauld, François VI, duc de la. *La Justification de l'amour*. Edited by J. D. Hubert. Paris: A.-G. Nizet, 1971.

Ronzeaud, Pierre, "La femme dans le roman utopique de la fin du XVIIᵉ siècle", pp. 79-98, *Onze Etudes sur l'image de la femme dans la littérature française du XVIIᵉ siècle*, ed. Wolfgang Leiner, Gunter Narr, Tübingen/Jean-Michel Place, Paris, 1984.

Rossum-Guyon, Françoise van. "Point de vue ou perspective narrative." *Poétique*, no. 4 (1970): 576-97.

Saintsbury, George. *A History of the French Novel*. London: MacMillan and Co., Limited, 1917.

Sakharoff, Micheline. "La Sous-Conversation dans *La Princesse de Clèves*, un anti-roman." *French Forum* 2 (1977): 121-33.

Sarlet, Claudette. "La Description des personnages dans *La Princesse de Clèves*." *XVIIᵉ siècle* 44 (1959): 186-200.

Schafer, Roy. "Narration in the Psychoanalytic Dialogue." *Critical Inquiry* 7 (1980): 29-53.

Scholes, Robert, and Robert Kellogg. *The Nature of Narrative*. New York: Oxford University Press, 1966.

Scott, J. W. "The 'Digressions' of the *Princesse de Clèves*." *French Studies* 11 (1957): 315-22.

Scudéry, Madeleine de. *Artamène ou le Grand Cyrus*. Paris: Barbin, 1653.

———. *Conversations sur divers sujets*. Amsterdam: Daniel du Fresne, 1682.

———. *Les Femmes illustres*. Paris: Antoine de Sommaville,

1642.

Segal, Erich, ed. *Greek Tragedy: Modern Essays in Criticism.* New York: Harper & Row, 1983.

Segrais, Jean-Regnault de. *Les Nouvelles françaises.* Paris: Antoine de Sommaville, 1656.

Segre, Cesare. *Structures and Time: Narration, Poetry, Models.* Trans. John Meddemmen. Chicago: University of Chicago Press, 1979.

Smith, Barbara Herrnstein. *On the Margins of Discourse: The Relation of Literature and Language.* Chicago: University of Chicago Press, 1979.

Spitzer, Leo. *Essays on Seventeenth-Century French Literature.* Cambridge: Cambridge University Press, 1983.

Stanzel, Franz. *A Theory of Narrative.* Cambridge: Cambridge University Press, 1979.

————. *Narrative Situations in the Novel: Tom Jones, Moby-Dick, The Ambassadors, Ulysses.* Trans. James P. Pusack. Bloomington: Indiana University Press, 1971.

Stauffenegger, Roger, "La femme et la religion en milieu protestant", pp. 45-56, *La Femme à l'époque moderne, XVIe-XVIIIe*, Actes du Colloque de 1984, Bulletin n^0 9, P.U.P.S., Paris, 1985.

Stevick, Philip. *The Theory of the Novel.* New York: The French Press, 1967.

Atrauch, Edward H. *Philosophy of literary Criticism: A Method of Literary Analysis and Interpretation.* Jericho, New York: Exposition Press, 1974.

Thibaudet, A. *Réflexions sur le roman.* Paris: Gallimard, 1938.

Tilley, Arthur. *The Decline of the Age of Louis XIV: French Literature 1687-1715.* 2nd ed. New York: Barnes & Noble, Inc., 1968.

Tondeur, Claire-Lise. *Voix de femmes: Ecritures de femmes dans la littérature française du XIX-XXe siècles.* Lanham: University Press of America, Inc., 1990.

Turnell, Martin. *The Novel in France: Mme de La Fayette, Laclos, Constant, Stendal, Balzac, Flaubert, Proust.* New

York: New Directions, 1951.

Venesoen, Constant. *Etudes sur la littérature féminine au XVIIe* siècle. Birmingham: Summa Publications, Inc, 1990.

Virmaux, Odette. *Les Héroïnes romanesques de Madame de LaFayette*. Paris: Klincksieck, 1981.

von Wright, Georg H. *Causality and Determinism*. New York: Columbia University Press, 1974.

Walcutt, Charles Child. *Man's Changing Mask, Modes and Methods of Characterization in Fiction*. Minneapolis: University of Minnesota Press, 1966.

Watt, Ian. *The Rise of the Novel*. Berkeley: University of California 1957.

Wells, Byron. "The King, the Court, the Country: Theme and Structure in *La Princesse de Clèves*." *Papers on French Seventeenth-Century Literature* 12, no. 23 (1985): 543-58.

White, Hayden. *The Content of the Form: Narrative Discourse and Historical Representation*. Baltimore: John Hopkins University Press, 1987.

———. "The Value of Narrativity in the Representation of Reality." *Critical Inquiry* 7 (1980): 5-27.

Williams, Charles G. S. *Madame de Sévigné*. Boston: Twayne Publishers, 1981.

Witcomb, Selden L. *The Study of a Novel*. Boston: D. C. Heath and Company, Publishers, 1905.

Zéraffa, Michel. *Roman et société*. Presses Universitaires de France, 1971.

Index[1]

---

[1]Numbers in boldface refer to pages devoted entirely to the
items that are also listed as subheadings within the text.

CONTEMPORARY CRITICAL CONCEPTS AND PRE-ENLIGHTENMENT LITERATURE

Writers who worked before the beginning of rationalist universalism's triumphal period—which may be ending now—explored issues of consciousness, ideology, and culture that recent criticism and critical theory, using various specialized vocabularies of concepts, have returned to the center of literary and social criticism. These early modern figures often anticipated some of our dilemmas: How to manipulate an apparently quite mutable world and, at the same time, preserve belief in an immutable "centered" self? How to reconcile rationalist universalism with personal and cultural stability? Rene Descartes' postulate of man as the master and proprietor of an increasingly *built* world is fundamentally incompatible with his effort to underwrite man as a stable philosophical subject. Man's technical and linguistic mastery devours his "transcendent subjectivity." Students of literature are now using the ideas of what I will call "post-enlightenment thinkers"—Max Horkheimer, Jacques Lacan, Michael Foucault, Rene Girard, and others—to elucidate the implicit and explicit debates about rationalism that are embedded in literary works.

This trend is most usefully seen as a renewal of contact with preoccupations that were quite current in medieval, Renaissance, and seventeenth-century European literature. To date, however, innovative criticism has focused on more recent literature. Some post-structuralists—most notably Jacques Lacan—have tried their hand at interpreting early works. Their ideas are interesting, but their knowledge of the periods in question is often weak.

Manuscripts on Elizabethan and Restoration theater, French, Italian, and German writers of the medieval and Renaissance periods, and the seventeenth-century French dramatists and moralists are welcome. Hamlet, The Tempest, Rabelais, Montaigne, Pascal, Molière, Dante—these and others would be excellent topics.

Dr. Larry Riggs, Department of Modern Foreign Languages
Butler University, 4600 Sunset Avenue, Indianapolis, IN 46208